A BREATH OF FRESH AIR
To Start Your Day

A BREATH OF FRESH AIR
To Start Your Day

RANDOLPH E. DANIELS, SR.

THE WRITING ON THE WALL
PUBLISHING SERVICES
ORLANDO, FL 32862, U.S.A.

Unless otherwise indicated, all Scriptural quotations are taken from the *Holy Bible,* New Living Translation, copyright © 1996, 2004. Used by permission of Tyndale House Publishers, Inc., Wheaton, Illinois 60189. All rights reserved. Scripture taken from the HOLY BIBLE, NEW INTERNATIONAL VERSION ®. Copyright © 1973, 1978, 1984 by International Bible Society. Used by permission of Zondervan. Scripture quotations marked KJV are from The Full Life Study Bible, King James Version Copyright © 1992 by Life Publishers International

A BREATH OF FRESH AIR To Start Your Day
Randolph E. Daniels, Sr.
P.O. Box 621433
Orlando, Florida 32862 – 1433
Website:
www.thewritingonthewal.wix.com/daisysdaniels
E-Mail address: thewritingonthewall@aol.com

Library of Congress Control Number: 2015908561

ISBN 978-0-9914002-5-6

Printed in the United States of America

INTRODUCTION

So encourage each other and build each other up,
just as you are already doing.

1 Thessalonians 5:11 NLT

➢ A new recruit of the Armed Services is in the midst of painstaking physical and academic training in boot camp. He is uncertain if he will make it through to see Graduation Day because the training is so demanding.

➢ An author is writing a new book based on a new and exciting subject. She is worried how the book will be received by the public because of the subject matter.

➢ A person who was unable to exercise regularly due to physical limitations is about to enter a serious exercise program. He is hesitant because of the past limitations.

➢ A runner is near the end of a long race; her legs ache, her throat is burning, and everything within her wants her to quit.

What is it that ties these people together? What is it that these folks have in common? They all need encouragement! Webster's New World Dictionary defines encourage as: *to give courage, hope, or confidence*. Each one of the aforementioned individuals need courage, hope, or confidence to complete the task that is before them. An encouraging word will give them the extra push they need to reach the finish line.

They are not the only ones that need encouragement. Everyone needs encouragement at some time or another. Life is like one long race; your legs ache, your throat burns, and everything within you tells you to just give up, throw in the towel, and quit. But an encouraging word will give you the courage, hope, and confidence to make it to your finish line.

Encouragement is emphasized throughout Scripture because it is necessary in our walk with God, and is essential for completing the purposes that He has for our lives.

➢ God instructed Moses to encourage Joshua, who was given the task of leading the children of Israel into the Promised Land.
➢ The prophets Haggai and Zechariah were instrumental in encouraging Zerubbabel in his efforts to rebuild the Temple of God.
➢ Nehemiah encouraged the people to continue their work to repair the wall surrounding Jerusalem.

As you can see, encouragement is very important to our Heavenly Father. So much so, it is one of the *spiritual gifts* that He provides to us in order to build each other up.

One of the greatest encouragers of all time was Barnabas. He was so encouraging that he earned the nickname "Son of Encouragement" from the Jerusalem Christians. Barnabas understood that an encouraging word could change someone's life. He was drawn to people he could encourage, and he was a great help to those around him. One of the best ways to help someone is to encourage them.

As I mentioned, everyone needs encouragement at some time or another. But, the *value* of encouragement is often missed because it tends to be private rather than public. People mostly need encouragement when they feel most alone. This is why we are *called* to encourage one another.

The enemy on the other hand, uses the opposite of encouragement to prevent us from accomplishing everything God has placed on our hearts to fulfill. He uses *discouragement.* Discouragement is a weapon the enemy uses in his attempts to deprive us of hope; deprive us of courage, and deprive us of confidence. All it takes is a discouraging word or action and we are stopped in our tracks. We can't go any further and we fall into a state of paralysis. This is why we should provide more encouragement and less criticism.

Another definition for encourage is: to make strong. The reason I wrote this book is because I want to encourage someone. I want to make you strong as you pursue whatever God has placed on your heart to do. Often times, King David had to encourage himself in life.

Therefore, I want you to use this book each day, as a tool to become like David and encourage yourself.

Life can be discouraging, stale, and flat, so I want you to begin each day with a *Breath of Fresh Air!*

To the glory of God!

Randolph E. Daniels, Sr.

And Saul was yet the more afraid of David; and
Saul became David's enemy continually.

1 Samuel 18:29 KJV

$$\left(\begin{array}{c} \text{The enemy doesn't fight you for} \\ \text{where you are, he fights you for} \\ \text{where you're going.} \end{array} \right)$$

1 Samuel 24:20 KJV

And now, behold, I know well that thou shalt surely
be king, and that the kingdom of Israel shall be
established in thine hand.

JANUARY 1

Some people place their trust in
their intellect, their wealth, or their
jobs, but these can be unreliable.
Our God richly gives us all we need
when we place our trust in Him. Is
your trust in the right place?

Some trust in chariots, and some in horses: but we
will remember the name of the LORD our God.

Psalm 20:7 KJV

JANUARY 2

> Being a child of the King does not
> EXCUSE us from troubles,
> but being His child does
> EMPOWER us to overcome
> troubles.
> BE EMPOWERED!

For whatsoever is born of God overcometh the world: and this is the victory that overcometh the world, even our faith.

1 John 5:4 KJV

JANUARY 3

Fight the good fight along with all
other believers. Take hold of eternal
life. You were chosen for it when
you openly told others what you
believe. Many witnesses heard you.

Fight the good fight of faith, lay hold on eternal life,
whereunto thou art also called, and hast professed a
good profession before many witnesses.

1 Timothy 6:12 KJV

[3]

JANUARY 4

Don't fret over what was lost in the past. Look to the future because the Lord is a God of retribution and He will repay in full!

Dearly beloved, avenge not yourselves, but rather give place unto wrath: for it is written, Vengeance is mine; I will repay, saith the Lord.

Romans 12:19 KJV

JANUARY 5

There is greatness within you! Your greatness is released by serving others. Out of love Jesus served us; out of love we should serve others. Tap into your greatness!

But he that is greatest among you shall be your servant.

Matthew 23:11 KJV

JANUARY 6

No matter the situation or
circumstance you're facing today,
the Lord will see you through. He
will help you, deliver you, and save
you because you trust Him!

You are my hiding place; you will protect me from
trouble and surround me with songs of deliverance.

Psalm 32:7 NIV

JANUARY 7

> God has given two unchangeable things: His promise and His oath. Through His promise and His oath God is saying, "I swear I will bless you!"

So God has given both his promise and his oath. These two things are unchangeable because it is impossible for God to lie. Therefore, we who have fled to him for refuge can have great confidence as we hold to the hope that lies before us.

Hebrews 6:18 NLT

JANUARY 8

God loves you with an everlasting love. A love that will never quit; a love that will never give up on you, so you should not give up on Him. God has not forgotten about you!

But God, who is rich in mercy, for his great love wherewith he loved us,

Ephesians 2:4 KJV

JANUARY 9

When you can't trust what your eyes see, you must rely on what your ears hear – the voice of God. Hold on to your faith. God IS who He says He is and He will DO what He said He would do. You're almost there!

So then faith cometh by hearing, and hearing by the word of God.

Romans 10:17 KJV

JANUARY 10

No matter how devastating or overwhelming the situation, we, as Kingdom Ambassadors, must always do what is right and trust God, who will NEVER fail us. Trust overcomes hate. He is Jehovah Shammah; He is right there in the worst situations with a promise and with hope.

It was round about eighteen thousand measures: and the name of the city from that day shall be, The LORD is there.

Ezekiel 48:35 KJV

JANUARY 11

Whatever you may be going through, rest assured your help is on the way. The Lord is watching over your life, and He'll make everything you're going through turn around in your favor. If it hasn't turned around, then He's not finished working it out. Hold on – a change is on the way!

The eyes of the Lord are upon the righteous, and his ears are open unto their cry.

Psalm 34:15 KJV

JANUARY 12

If it had not been for the Lord! He did it before in your life and He will do it again! The Lord was on our side. Otherwise, the enemy attack would have killed us all, because it was furious.

If it had not been the LORD who was on our side, when men rose up against us: Then they had swallowed us up quick, when their wrath was kindled against us:

Psalm 124:2 -3 KJV

JANUARY 13

May God fill you with the
knowledge of His will through all
the wisdom and understanding that
the Spirit gives. May you be made
strong with all the strength which
comes from His glorious power, so
that you may be able to endure
everything with patience.
In the name of Jesus!

Strengthened with all might, according to his
glorious power, unto all patience and longsuffering
with joyfulness;

Colossians 1:11 KJV

[13]

JANUARY 14

It is your Father's good pleasure to give you the kingdom. Your Father enjoys blessing you!

"So don't be afraid, little flock. For it gives your Father great happiness to give you the Kingdom."

Luke 12:32 NLT

JANUARY 15

> God knows the way you take. When
> He has tested you, you shall come
> forth as gold.

But he knoweth the way that I take: when he hath
tried me, I shall come forth as gold.

Job 23:10 KJV

JANUARY 16

Be encouraged, something good is
going to happen to you today!

Wherefore comfort yourselves together, and edify
one another, even as also ye do.

1 Thessalonians 5:11 KJV

JANUARY 17

> If God be for you and His Spirit
> dwells within you, there is nothing
> you can't do; conquer and
> overcome!

What shall we then say to these things? If God be
for us, who can be against us?

Romans 8:31 KJV

JANUARY 18

God's presence will accompany you through the good times and bad times. And that is something to be thankful for.

In every thing give thanks: for this is the will of God in Christ Jesus concerning you.

1 Thessalonians 5:18 KJV

JANUARY 19

$$\left\{ \begin{array}{l} \text{Take delight IN His presence, and} \\ \text{don't despair IN your problems.} \end{array} \right\}$$

In him our hearts rejoice, for we trust in his holy name.

Psalm 33:21 NLT

JANUARY 20

Hold on to the Lord. He's your praise and your God, who has done great things in your life that you have seen with your own eyes.

You must fear the LORD your God and worship him and cling to him. Your oaths must be in his name alone. He alone is your God, the only one who is worthy of your praise, the one who has done these mighty miracles that you have seen with your own eyes.

Deuteronomy 10:20 – 21 NLT

JANUARY 21

Regardless if it's been a year or two years, what God promised you – He has every intention of bringing it to pass. Don't get weary!

And let us not be weary in well doing: for in due season we shall reap, if we faint not.

Galatians 6:9 KJV

JANUARY 22

Doubt and unbelief are strategies of the enemy to weaken your faith. I rebuke doubt and unbelief in your life, and pray that your faith may not fail. In Jesus name!

And immediately Jesus stretched forth his hand, and caught him, and said unto him, O thou of little faith, wherefore didst thou doubt?

Matthew 14:31 KJV

JANUARY 23

> Not one of God's good promises to
> you will fail; every one will be
> fulfilled! For all the promises of God
> in Him are Yes, and in Him Amen,
> unto the glory of God by us.

For all the promises of God in him are yea, and in
him Amen, unto the glory of God by us.

2 Corinthians 1:20 KJV

JANUARY 24

God knows EVERYTHING you're
going through. Not only does He
know, but He also cares! Cast your
care upon Him for He cares for you.

Give all your worries and cares to God, for he cares
about you.

1 Peter 5:7 NLT

JANUARY 25

> God doesn't give us all the details of
> the plans He has for our lives,
> because He wants us to go through
> the process of trusting Him; to get
> us to the expected end. Trust Him!

"For I know the plans I have for you," says the
Lord.

Jeremiah 29:11a NLT

JANUARY 26

God was not having a bad day when He created you. You are fearfully and wonderfully made. Embrace your "YOU"niqueness!

I will praise thee; for I am fearfully and wonderfully made: marvellous are thy works; and that my soul knoweth right well.

Psalm 139:14 KJV

JANUARY 27

I pray God gives you a sign of His goodness that is so great your enemies may see it and be put to shame! How great is the goodness that God has reserved for those who honor Him; blessing them before the watching world.

How great is the goodness you have stored up for those who fear you. You lavish it on those who come to you for protection, blessing them before the watching world.

Psalm 31:19 NLT

JANUARY 28

Don't throw in the towel – you can make it. Go the distance!

I returned, and saw under the sun, that the race is not to the swift, nor the battle to the strong, neither yet bread to the wise, nor yet riches to men of understanding, nor yet favour to men of skill; but time and chance happeneth to them all.

Ecclesiastes 9:11 KJV

JANUARY 29

Hold on – your breakthrough is coming – any day now!

For the vision is yet for an appointed time, but at the end it shall speak, and not lie: though it tarry, wait for it; because it will surely come, it will not tarry.

Habakkuk 2:3 KJV

JANUARY 30

The road to prosperity is paved by
giving (your time, talent, resources)
not by getting. Be a blessing to
someone today!

Give, and it shall be given unto you; good measure,
pressed down, and shaken together, and running
over, shall men give into your bosom. For with the
same measure that ye mete withal it shall be
measured to you again.

Luke 6:38 KJV

JANUARY 31

{ You ain't seen nothing yet! }

For since the beginning of the world men have not heard, nor perceived by the ear, neither hath the eye seen, O God, beside thee, what he hath prepared for him that waiteth for him.

Isaiah 64:4 KJV

FEBRUARY 1

God reigns over my circumstances
so my problems don't stand a
chance!

The LORD reigneth, he is clothed with majesty;
the LORD is clothed with strength, wherewith he
hath girded himself: the world also is stablished,
that it cannot be moved.

Psalm 93:1 KJV

FEBRUARY 2

It's already getting better!

Anyone who is among the living has hope—even a live dog is better off than a dead lion!

Ecclesiastes 9:4 KJV

FEBRUARY 3

You can't give up in the middle of
the fight. Keep pressing for your
blessing!

I press on toward the goal to win the prize for which
God has called me heavenward in Christ Jesus.

Philippians 3:14 KJV

FEBRUARY 4

Jesus became low so I can fly high!
~ Fly Like An Eagle

But we see Jesus, who was made a little lower than the angels for the suffering of death, crowned with glory and honour; that he by the grace of God should taste death for every man.

Hebrews 2:9 KJV

FEBRUARY 5

God is _____.
(You fill in the blank)

God thundereth marvellously with his voice; great things doeth he, which we cannot comprehend.

Job 37:5 KJV

FEBRUARY 6

$$\Bigl(\quad\text{Exercise your brain...you're the}\\ \text{"head" not the tail!}\quad\Bigr)$$

And the LORD shall make thee the head, and not the tail; and thou shalt be above only, and thou shalt not be beneath; if that thou hearken unto the commandments of the LORD thy God, which I command thee this day, to observe and to do them:

Deuteronomy 28:13 KJV

FEBRUARY 7

The Kingdom of God is within you
and wherever you go you bring light
to dark places!

Ye are all the children of light, and the children of
the day: we are not of the night, nor of darkness.

1 Thessalonians 5:5 KJV

FEBRUARY 8

Avoid debt – you're the lender and
not the borrower!

The rich ruleth over the poor, and the borrower is
servant to the lender.

Proverbs 22:7 KJV

FEBRUARY 9

{
If you're not changing, you're stuck.
And if you're stuck, you're not
moving forward!
}

But his wife looked back from behind him, and she
became a pillar of salt.

Genesis 19:26 KJV

FEBRUARY 10

When the enemy comes to collect payment tell Him, "I don't owe you! My account has been PAID IN FULL!"

In whom we have redemption through his blood, the forgiveness of sins, according to the riches of his grace;

Ephesians 1:7 KJV

[41]

FEBRUARY 11

At times you may stumble and fall,
but regardless of your mistakes,
God will not take His love from
you. Nor will He ever betray His
faithfulness. He will maintain His
love for you forever.

Nor height, nor depth, nor any other creature, shall
be able to separate us from the love of God, which
is in Christ Jesus our Lord.

Romans 8:39 KJV

FEBRUARY 12

You are a child of the Most High
God. A child of the Most HIGH
cannot allow themselves to be
brought LOW as a result of
unforgiveness. Forgiveness gives
YOU the power, and releases you
from that place of pain.

Forgive as your Father in heaven has forgiven you!

Colossians 3:13 KJV

FEBRUARY 13

{
DECLARE THIS:
"If God hadn't been there for me, I
never would have made it." Now
thank Him for what He has done!
}

God is our refuge and strength, a very present help
in trouble.

Psalm 46:1 KJV

FEBRUARY 14

When doubts fill your mind, and
your heart is in turmoil, God will
quiet your spirit and give you
renewed hope!

And he said unto them, Why are ye troubled? and
why do thoughts arise in your hearts?

Luke 24:38 KJV

FEBRUARY 15

When you are upset and beside
yourself, God's comfort will calm
you down and cheer you up!

And Jesus answered and said unto her, Martha,
Martha, thou art careful and troubled about many
things:

Luke 10:41 KJV

FEBRUARY 16

When you are worried about many
things, God's assuring words will
soothe your soul. So don't be
anxious about tomorrow. God will
take care of your tomorrow too.
Live one day at a time.

Take therefore no thought for the morrow: for the
morrow shall take thought for the things of itself.
Sufficient unto the day is the evil thereof.

Matthew 6:34 KJV

FEBRUARY 17

{
When you are overwhelmed by the
cares of life, God's comfort will
bring you joy!
}

Nevertheless I tell you the truth; It is expedient for
you that I go away: for if I go not away, the
Comforter will not come unto you; but if I depart, I
will send him unto you.

John 16:7 KJV

FEBRUARY 18

When you are burdened with
worries, God will comfort you and
make you feel secure!

Come unto me, all ye that labour and are heavy
laden, and I will give you rest.

Matthew 11:28 KJV

FEBRUARY 19

One of the great things about God's
benefits is: you can't be denied
because of pre-existing conditions!

Bless the LORD, O my soul, and forget not all his
benefits:

Psalm 103:2 KJV

FEBRUARY 20

You may have hit a road block or an obstacle in your life. How you respond to the obstacle or roadblock will determine your future.

Now I beseech you, brethren, mark them which cause divisions and offences contrary to the doctrine which ye have learned; and avoid them.

Romans 16:17 KJV

FEBRUARY 21

God knows how much you can bear.
When you've carried all you can,
God will carry what you can't.

Blessed be the Lord, who daily loadeth us with benefits, even the God of our salvation. Selah.

Psalm 68:19 KJV

FEBRUARY 22

After this – God's going to perfect
you, settle you, strengthen you, and
establish you!

But the God of all grace, who hath called us unto
his eternal glory by Christ Jesus, after that ye have
suffered a while, make you perfect, stablish,
strengthen, settle you.

1 Peter 5:10 KJV

[53]

FEBRUARY 23

Whatever you're in need of…God's got it today!

But my God shall supply all your need according to his riches in glory by Christ Jesus.

Philippians 4:19 KJV

FEBRUARY 24

> Look at this day with a sense of
> excitement; a sense of optimism; a
> sense of wonder and joy at the
> possibilities of this new day!

In God we boast all the day long, and praise thy
name for ever. Selah.

Psalm 44:8 KJV

FEBRUARY 25

Hang in there! Things are going to get better. God is doing something specifically for you!

Behold, I will do a new thing; now it shall spring forth; shall ye not know it? I will even make a way in the wilderness, and rivers in the desert.

Isaiah 43:19 KJV

FEBRUARY 26

How interested is God in you? He counts the hairs on your head. You are that precious to Him!

But the very hairs of your head are all numbered.

Matthew 10:30 KJV

FEBRUARY 27

Learn to trust God and know that as long as you're doing your best, you are exactly where you are supposed to be.

And whatsoever ye do, do it heartily, as to the Lord, and not unto men;

Colossians 3:23 KJV

FEBRUARY 28

You may not understand it, it may not seem fair, but God knows what He is doing.

For my thoughts are not your thoughts, neither are your ways my ways, saith the LORD.

Isaiah 55:8 KJV

FEBRUARY 29

Your destiny is too great; your
assignment is too important; your
time is too valuable. Don't let fear
intimidate you.

For God hath not given us the spirit of fear; but of
power, and of love, and of a sound mind.

2 Timothy 1:7 KJV

MARCH 1

God doesn't always let us take the easy way. Sometimes He takes us through hills, valleys, and detours.

Better is the end of a thing than the beginning thereof: and the patient in spirit is better than the proud in spirit.

Ecclesiastes 7:8 KJV

MARCH 2

When a door closes, it may seem
like a disappointment. But, that' may
be another step to your divine
destiny.

And hope maketh not ashamed; because the love of
God is shed abroad in our hearts by the Holy Ghost
which is given unto us.

Romans 5:5 KJV

MARCH 3

DECLARE THIS:
"In spite of the pain; in spite of the adversity, I'm still in the game."

That thou mayest give him rest from the days of adversity, until the pit be digged for the wicked.

Psalm 94:13 KJV

MARCH 4

Even when the odds are stacked
against you, trust in the Lord's
goodness and favor. And see Him
come through for you.

Trust in the LORD with all thine heart; and lean not
unto thine own understanding. In all thy ways
acknowledge him, and he shall direct thy paths.

Proverbs 3:5 – 6 KJV

MARCH 5

God is in complete control. So be a
prisoner of hope. Get up each day
expecting His favor.

For we through the Spirit wait for the hope of
righteousness by faith.

Galatians 5:5 KJV

MARCH 6

God is working behind the SCENE
on things that are about to show up
and be SEEN.
Question is...are you ready?
And will you recognize it?

Even the mystery which hath been hid from ages
and from generations, but now is made manifest to
his saints:

Colossians 1:26 KJV

MARCH 7

Your problems may be big, but our
God is much bigger. Your obstacles
may be high, but we serve
the Most High God.

I will cry unto God most high; unto God that
performeth all things for me.

Psalm 57:2 KJV

MARCH 8

Instead of being overwhelmed by burdens, believe that you're going to be overwhelmed by God's blessings.

And all these blessings shall come on thee, and overtake thee, if thou shalt hearken unto the voice of the LORD thy God.

Deuteronomy 28:2 KJV

MARCH 9

Choose today what you will be: You
can be pitiful or
you can be powerful.
You can't be both.

Behold, I give unto you power to tread on serpents
and scorpions, and over all the power of the enemy:
and nothing shall by any means hurt you.

Luke 10:19 KJV

MARCH 10

Many large corporations are considered too big to fail, yet they fail anyway. But God, who created the heaven and earth never fails because He truly is TOO BIG TO FAIL!

In the year that king Uzziah died I saw also the LORD sitting upon a throne, high and lifted up, and his train filled the temple.

Isaiah 6:1 KJV

MARCH 11

Make a decision to keep pressing forward, keep believing, and keep stretching until you see your dream fulfilled.

Come now therefore, and let us slay him, and cast him into some pit, and we will say, Some evil beast hath devoured him: and we shall see what will become of his dreams.

Genesis 37:20 KJV

MARCH 12

Let haters hate – they have nothing
else to do – for if they did, they
wouldn't have time to notice what
you're doing.

And about the eleventh hour he went out, and found
others standing idle, and saith unto them, Why stand
ye here all the day idle?

Matthew 20:6 KJV

MARCH 13

{
God has promised: if you'll turn
matters over to Him and let Him
handle them His way, He'll make
your wrongs right.
}

Righteousness and justice are the foundation of
your throne.

MARCH 14

People look on the outside. God
looks on the heart. God knows what
you are capable of. You're capable
of doing great exploits because you
know your GOD!

But the LORD said unto Samuel, Look not on his
countenance, or on the height of his stature; because
I have refused him: for the LORD seeth not as man
seeth; for man looketh on the outward appearance,
but the LORD looketh on the heart.

1 Samuel 16:7 KJV

MARCH 15

Today, no matter what battle you
may be facing, declare and celebrate
the freedom and peace that Jesus
promised.

If the Son therefore shall make you free, ye shall be
free indeed.

John 8:36 KJV

MARCH 16

You give life to your faith by what
you say. Declare victory. Declare
health. Declare favor.

And Jesus said unto them, Because of your
unbelief: for verily I say unto you, If ye have faith
as a grain of mustard seed, ye shall say unto this
mountain, Remove hence to yonder place; and it
shall remove; and nothing shall be impossible unto
you.

Matthew 17:20 KJV

MARCH 17

God will make your wrongs right.
He wants to repay you for every
unfairness. He is a God of justice.

And the heavens shall declare his righteousness: for
God is judge himself. Selah.

Psalm 50:6 KJV

MARCH 18

{
Today, find something
to be grateful for.
Every day is a gift from God.
}

But I, with shouts of grateful praise, will sacrifice to you. What I have vowed I will make good. I will say, 'Salvation comes from the Lord.

Jonah 2:9 NIV

MARCH 19

You may have obstacles in your path, but the good news is, the Power that is for you is greater than any power against you.

Ye are of God, little children, and have overcome them: because greater is he that is in you, than he that is in the world.

1 John 4:4 KJV

MARCH 20

Take the limits off of God. He wants
to do something new;
something amazing
in your life.

Thou hast heard, see all this; and will not ye declare
it? I have shewed thee new things from this time,
even hidden things, and thou didst not know them.

Isaiah 48:6 KJV

MARCH 21

> Don't live life comparing yourself to
> everyone else. God has created you
> to be you, and you are free to be
> yourself!

For we dare not make ourselves of the number, or
compare ourselves with some that commend
themselves: but they measuring themselves by
themselves, and comparing themselves among
themselves, are not wise.

2 Corinthians 10:12 KJV

MARCH 22

DECLARE THIS:
"I believe doors are opening for me today that no one can close, and favor surrounds me like a shield. In Jesus' Name!"

For thou, LORD, wilt bless the righteous; with favour wilt thou compass him as with a shield.

Psalm 5:12 KJV

MARCH 23

Believe that no matter what has come against you, no matter how unfair it was, things are shifting in your favor.

For the mountains shall depart, and the hills be removed; but my kindness shall not depart from thee, neither shall the covenant of my peace be removed, saith the LORD that hath mercy on thee.

Isaiah 54:10 KJV

MARCH 24

DECLARE THIS:
"I'm above only today – above the
devil, above fear, above poverty,
and above 'just getting by'. I'm the
head and not the tail!"

There is no fear in love; but perfect love casteth out
fear: because fear hath torment. He that feareth is
not made perfect in love.

1 John 4:18 KJV

MARCH 25

$$\left(\begin{array}{c} \text{Diligence is God's order to keep me} \\ \text{faithful, fruitful, focused, and keep} \\ \text{me from falling.} \end{array} \right)$$

Keep thy heart with all diligence; for out of it are the issues of life.

Proverbs 4:24 KJV

MARCH 26

DECLARE THIS:
"God has given me authority over
ALL the power of the enemy.
Nothing shall harm or defeat me. In
Jesus' Name!"

If ye shall ask any thing in my name, I will do it.

John 14:14 KJV

MARCH 27

{
DECLARE THIS:
"I expect divine protection,
provision, and promotion because I
am in a covenant with God through
the blood of Jesus!"
}

But now hath he obtained a more excellent ministry, by how much also he is the mediator of a better covenant, which was established upon better promises.

Hebrews 8:6 KJV

MARCH 28

DECLARE THIS:
"I am in God's presence by the
blood of Jesus, and His presence is
in me! I'll never be lonely another
day in my life!"

Cast me not away from thy presence; and take not
thy holy spirit from me.

Psalm 51:11 KJV

MARCH 29

God knew me before He formed me.
Destiny Prayer:
Lord, help me to KNOW
what you KNEW!

Before I formed thee in the belly I knew thee; and before thou camest forth out of the womb I sanctified thee, and I ordained thee a prophet unto the nations.

Jeremiah 1:5 KJV

MARCH 30

> Trouble thought it was coming to
> destroy you, but it was actually
> coming to be introduced to your
> faith.
> ~ Awesome God!

But we have this treasure in earthen vessels, that the excellency of the power may be of God, and not of us. We are troubled on every side, yet not distressed; we are perplexed, but not in despair; Persecuted, but not forsaken; cast down, but not destroyed;

2 Corinthians 4:7 – 9 KJV

MARCH 31

$$\left[\text{Get into agreement with God!} \right]$$

Can two walk together, except they be agreed?

Amos 3:3 KJV

APRIL 1

$$\Bigg\{ \text{God never changes, but He can change anything! All things are possible with God.} \Bigg\}$$

Jesus Christ the same yesterday, and today, and for ever.

Hebrews 13:8 KJV

APRIL 2

It may not have happened in the
past, but it can still happen in your
future. God is still
on the throne.

The LORD hath prepared his throne in the heavens;
and his kingdom ruleth over all.

Psalm 103:19 KJV

APRIL 3

$$\left(\begin{array}{c}\text{DECLARE THIS:}\\ \text{"God knows what's headed my way}\\ \text{today. He has a plan. He will}\\ \text{provide and protect me, in Jesus'}\\ \text{Name!"}\end{array}\right)$$

For the LORD knoweth the way of the righteous: but the way of the ungodly shall perish.

Psalm 1:6 KJV

APRIL 4

$$\left\{ \begin{array}{c} \text{Don't settle for mediocrity when God} \\ \text{has put greatness in you.} \end{array} \right\}$$

But it shall not be so among you: but whosoever will be great among you, let him be your minister;

Matthew 20:26 KJV

APRIL 5

$$\left(\begin{array}{c} \text{When fear knocks, let faith answer} \\ \text{the door. Don't give those thoughts} \\ \text{of fear the time of day.} \end{array}\right)$$

Therefore will not we fear, though the earth be removed, and though the mountains be carried into the midst of the sea;

Psalm 46:2 KJV

APRIL 6

{
Jesus has already nailed your past,
pain, and problems to the cross.
It's OVER!
}

Blotting out the handwriting of ordinances that was against us, which was contrary to us, and took it out of the way, nailing it to his cross;

Colossians 2:14 KJV

APRIL 7

Remember to count your blessings
and not your troubles.

Giving thanks always for all things unto God and
the Father in the name of our Lord Jesus Christ;

Ephesians 5:20 KJV

APRIL 8

Serving God doesn't mean we'll no longer have difficulties. We're still on the battlefield, but we don't have to fight alone.

Who is this King of glory? The Lord strong and mighty, the Lord mighty in battle.

Psalm 24:8 NIV

APRIL 9

The way God sees it, you are stronger than your struggle. The battle is getting you to believe it.

Praise the Lord, who is my rock. He trains my hands for war and gives my fingers skill for battle.

Psalm 144:1 NLT

APRIL 10

> Our feelings are real and they are powerful, but they are not more powerful than God and truth.

And ye shall know the truth, and the truth shall make you free.

John 8:32 KJV

APRIL 11

$\Big($ When God assigns an impossible task to you, all you have to say is, "Be it unto me!" $\Big)$

And Mary said, Behold the handmaid of the Lord; be it unto me according to thy word. And the angel departed from her.

Luke 1:38 KJV

APRIL 12

You can feel afraid, but you don't have to be afraid – God is with you.

But Jesus immediately said to them: "Take courage! It is I. Don't be afraid."

Matthew 14:27 NIV

APRIL 13

DECLARE THIS:
"I refuse to give others the power to control my emotions or my day. I choose to walk in the spirit!"

A fool uttereth all his mind: but a wise man keepeth it in till afterwards.

Proverbs 29:11 KJV

APRIL 14

Love is the most powerful force in the Universe because God is Love! And that powerful force loves you.

He that loveth not knoweth not God; for God is love.

1 John 4:8 KJV

APRIL 15

You may be having a "Job" kind of day where everything that could go wrong is going wrong. Rest assured things will change. God always causes you to triumph!

Many are the afflictions of the righteous: but the LORD delivereth him out of them all.

Psalm 34:19 KJV

APRIL 16

$$\left\{\begin{array}{c} \text{DECLARE THIS:} \\ \text{``I know what's in my future is} \\ \text{greater than what's in my past.''} \end{array}\right\}$$

Behold, the former things are come to pass, and new things do I declare: before they spring forth I tell you of them.

Isaiah 42:9 KJV

APRIL 17

> Our God is a God of increase, not
> decrease. What are you believing for
> today?

And he increased his people greatly; and made them
stronger than their enemies.

Psalm 105:24 KJV

APRIL 18

DECLARE THIS:
"I am above ONLY and not
beneath! Because I am seated with
Christ, I expect ONLY victory
today. In Jesus' Name!"

And hath raised us up together, and made us sit
together in heavenly places in Christ Jesus:

Ephesians 2:6 KJV

APRIL 19

{
The Lord Himself watches over
you! He keeps watch over you as
you come and go, both now and
forever.
}

The LORD is thy keeper: the LORD is thy shade
upon thy right hand.
The LORD shall preserve thy going out and thy
coming in from this time forth, and even for
evermore.

Psalm 121:5, 8 KJV

APRIL 20

Make up your mind that you're not
going to quit until you see the fruit
of what God has placed within you.

And sow the fields, and plant vineyards, which may
yield fruits of increase.

Psalm 107:37 KJV

APRIL 21

{
Adam fell but Jesus rose. You sit
with the risen Savior in heavenly
places!
}

But there is a great difference between Adam's sin
and God's gracious gift. For the sin of this one man,
Adam, brought death to many. But even greater is
God's wonderful grace and his gift of forgiveness to
many through this other man, Jesus Christ.

Romans 5:15

APRIL 22

$$\left[\begin{array}{c} \text{Always remember and never forget:} \\ \text{God is FOR YOU!} \end{array}\right]$$

My little children, these things write I unto you, that ye sin not. And if any man sin, we have an advocate with the Father, Jesus Christ the righteous:

1 John 2:1 KJV

APRIL 23

$$\left\{ \begin{array}{c} \text{Do not pay back evil with evil or} \\ \text{cursing with cursing; instead, pay it} \\ \text{back with a blessing.} \\ \sim \text{Blessings!} \end{array} \right\}$$

Not rendering evil for evil, or railing for railing: but contrariwise blessing; knowing that ye are thereunto called, that ye should inherit a blessing.

1 Peter 3:9 KJV

APRIL 24

[LIVE!   ]

I shall not die, but live, and declare the works of the LORD.

Psalm 118:17 KJV

APRIL 25

Experiencing trials in your life is not a sign that you have lost favor with God; it is sign that you are experiencing life. Sometimes hardship comes as a result of obeying God.

That same day Pharaoh sent this order to the Egyptian slave drivers and the Israelite foremen: "Do not supply any more straw for making bricks. Make the people get it themselves! But still require them to make the same number of bricks as before. Don't reduce the quota. They are lazy. That's why they are crying out, 'Let us go and offer sacrifices to our God.' Load them down with more work. Make them sweat! That will teach them to listen to lies!"

Exodus 5:6 – 9 NLT

APRIL 26

{

DECLARE THIS:
"Today is a good day because God
is leaning in my direction. I will
take advantage of God's favor and
make something happen today!"

}

Behold, O God our shield, and look upon the face of thine anointed.

Psalm 84:9 KJV

APRIL 27

DECLARE THIS:
"Our God is the Great I AM, and
through His love I was created in
His likeness. And now I am. I am
the head and not the tail; I am
above and not beneath; I am healed;
I am delivered; I am set free and
I am...grateful!
Thank you, Lord!"

I am crucified with Christ: nevertheless I live; yet
not I, but Christ liveth in me: and the life which I
now live in the flesh I live by the faith of the Son of
God, who loved me, and gave himself for me.

Galatians 2:20 KJV

APRIL 28

$$\left(\begin{array}{c} \text{I DECLARE AND DECREE:} \\ \text{Everything about you is about to} \\ \text{shift!} \end{array}\right)$$

And he hath put a new song in my mouth, even praise unto our God: many shall see it, and fear, and shall trust in the LORD.

Psalm 40:3 KJV

APRIL 29

What God has for you will not only bless you, but it will glorify Him. Be patient. Your blessing may be deferred, but it has not been declined!

Rest in the Lord, and wait patiently for him.

Psalm 37:7 KJV

APRIL 30

Never allow your experiences to affect your expectations. Just because it didn't happen in the past, doesn't mean it won't happen in the future.

My soul, wait thou only upon God; for my expectation is from him.

Psalm 62:5 KJV

MAY 1

What happens to the real you if
you're a copy of someone else?
Be you!
You are an original!

For we are his workmanship, created in Christ Jesus
unto good works, which God hath before ordained
that we should walk in them.

Ephesians 2:10 KJV

MAY 2

DECLARE THIS:
"I will work hard to reach my goals
because hard work brings
abundance, but mere talk leads to
lack."
Work it out!

In all labour there is profit: but the talk of the lips
tendeth only to penury.

Proverbs 14:23 KJV

MAY 3

> In order to heal, we must first
> forgive. And sometimes the person
> we must forgive is ourselves.
> ~ Forgiveness!

But now we are delivered from the law, that being
dead wherein we were held; that we should serve in
newness of spirit, and not in the oldness of the
letter.

Romans 7:6 KJV

MAY 4

Your current situation is not
an indication of your
future destination!

Pharaoh sent for Joseph at once, and he was quickly
brought from the prison. After he shaved and
changed his clothes, he went in and stood before
Pharaoh.

Genesis 41:14 NLT

MAY 5

An angel from God may cross your path today. Be nice to strangers because some people have entertained angels without knowing it.

Be not forgetful to entertain strangers: for thereby some have entertained angels unawares.

Hebrews 13:2 KJV

MAY 6

Our God is not a random God. He is
a precise God. He has lined up
solutions for you – down to the very
second.

And we know that all things work together for good
to them that love God, to them who are the called
according to his purpose.

Romans 8:28 KJV

MAY 7

> DECLARE THIS:
> "I expect abundance today because Jesus came to give me an abundant life. He is the God of MORE than enough!"

The thief cometh not, but for to steal, and to kill, and to destroy: I am come that they might have life, and that they might have it more abundantly.

John 10:10 KJV

MAY 8

Put your shoulders back, hold your head high. The same power that raised Christ from the dead lives on the inside of you.

But if the Spirit of him that raised up Jesus from the dead dwell in you, he that raised up Christ from the dead shall also quicken your mortal bodies by his Spirit that dwelleth in you.

Romans 8:11 KJV

MAY 9

> DECLARE THIS:
> "God will make a way for me when it seems like there is no way. Jesus is the ONLY way, and He will make my way straight today!"

There hath no temptation taken you but such as is common to man: but God is faithful, who will not suffer you to be tempted above that ye are able; but will with the temptation also make a way to escape, that ye may be able to bear it.

1 Corinthians 10:13 KJV

MAY 10

HE is faithful and just! He has always been faithful and just; He will always be faithful and just!

Faithful is he that calleth you, who also will do it.

1 Thessalonians 5:24 KJV

MAY 11

Remaining calm in adversity is a
sign of great spiritual strength. No
matter what's going on in your life
right now, hold your peace!

But let patience have her perfect work, that ye may
be perfect and entire, wanting nothing.

James 1:4 KJV

MAY 12

Your faith is to be unshakable when everything around you is undependable. Believe that God's purpose in your life will come to pass regardless of whatever is going on around you.

There was a man in the land of Uz, whose name was Job; and that man was perfect and upright, and one that feared God, and eschewed evil.

Job 1:1 KJV

MAY 13

God is NEVER intimidated by the size of a problem. He is BIGGER than any problem. Place your trust in Him and He will lead you to victory!

Now unto him that is able to do exceeding abundantly above all that we ask or think, according to the power that worketh in us,

Ephesians 3:20 KJV

MAY 14

> Don't waste time mourning over
> something that God has rejected.
> Look to the future where God has
> something much greater in store for
> you!

For surely there is an end; and thine expectation
shall not be cut off.

Proverbs 23:18 KJV

MAY 15

You face many troubles – pain, grief, loss, sorrow, and sometimes failure. God promises to be your source of power, courage, and wisdom to help you through the problems.

You have given me your shield of victory. Your right hand supports me; your help has made me great.

Psalm 18:35 KJV

MAY 16

Faith doesn't believe what it sees...faith believes what was heard. Faith is acting on what God said without evidence that it's going to happen. Stand firm in your faith. God is the faithful God; keeping His covenant of love with those who love Him!

Stand therefore, having your loins girt about with truth, and having on the breastplate of righteousness;

Ephesians 6:14 KJV

MAY 17

Your footsteps are guided by His
word, which means the enemy
cannot stop you from reaching your
destiny. Keep walking and don't
look back!

The steps of a good man are ordered by the Lord:
and he delighteth in his way.

Psalm 37:23 KJV

MAY 18

Don't allow negative thoughts to
terrorize you. Think on whatsoever
things are true, honest, just, pure,
lovely, and are of good report; if
there be any virtue, and if there be
any praise, think on these things.
~ Free Your Mind

Finally, brethren, whatsoever things are true,
whatsoever things are honest, whatsoever things are
just, whatsoever things are pure, whatsoever things
are lovely, whatsoever things are of good report; if
there be any virtue, and if there be any praise, think
on these things.

Philippians 4:8 KJV

MAY 19

{
You can remain in bed to dream
dreams or you can get up to pursue
them. The choice is yours!
}

How long wilt thou sleep, O sluggard? when wilt
thou arise out of thy sleep?

Proverbs 6:9 KJV

MAY 20

{
Kindness is not weakness – it is the strength to love. Show someone how strong you are by showing some kindness today!
}

"By this everyone will know that you are my disciples, if you love one another."

John 13:15 KJV

MAY 21

$$\left(\begin{array}{c} \text{Don't leave your life up to chance.} \\ \text{Bet it all on red – the precious blood} \\ \text{of Jesus.} \end{array} \right)$$

But now you have been united with Christ Jesus. Once you were far away from God, but now you have been brought near to him through the blood of Christ.

Ephesians 2:13 KJV

MAY 22

God's grace is sufficient for you.
His Grace will not remove what
you're going through, but it will
strengthen you to endure it.

And he said unto me, My grace is sufficient for
thee: for my strength is made perfect in weakness.
Most gladly therefore will I rather glory in my
infirmities, that the power of Christ may rest upon
me.

2 Corinthians 12:9 KJV

MAY 23

Animals know exactly where to seek refuge when they are under attack from their enemies. When you're under attack, your place of refuge is in the shelter of the Most High! Dwell in it! Abide in it!

He that dwelleth in the secret place of the most High shall abide under the shadow of the Almighty.

Psalm 91:1 KJV

MAY 24

JESUS is the answer – now apply the question! Jesus can answer any question you may have regarding healing, deliverance, salvation, finances, family, and relationships.

Wherefore, holy brethren, partakers of the heavenly calling, consider the Apostle and High Priest of our profession, Christ Jesus;

Hebrews 3:1 KJV

MAY 25

Life is a series of adjustments. If
you don't adjust – life will provide
an adjustment for you. Take
authority over your life!

For to be carnally minded is death; but to be
spiritually minded is life and peace.

Romans 8:6 KJV

MAY 26

Sometimes folk will do things to you to see how you will react. Don't let them push your buttons. One of the advantages of having the fruit of the Spirit is: self control.

But the fruit of the Spirit is love, joy, peace, forbearance, kindness, goodness, faithfulness, gentleness and self-control. Against such things there is no law.

Galatians 5:22 KJV

MAY 27

The odds may be stacked against
you, but with God EVEN the ODDS
will turn in your favor!
~ He's Sovereign!

The Lord shall cause thine enemies that rise up
against thee to be smitten before thy face: they shall
come out against thee one way, and flee before thee
seven ways.

Deuteronomy 28:7 KJV

MAY 28

Are you a Saul, who looks to please the people or are you a David, who looks to please Almighty God?

So then they that are in the flesh cannot please God.

Romans 8:8 KJV

MAY 29

Everything you're going through
NOW, while no one is around, will
LATER be revealed before the
people for God's glory!

Fear them not therefore: for there is nothing
covered, that shall not be revealed; and hid, that
shall not be known.

Matthew 10:26 KJV

MAY 30

$$\left\{ \begin{array}{c} \text{God is no respecter of persons. If He} \\ \text{blessed Abraham, Isaac, and Jacob,} \\ \text{He will bless you!} \end{array} \right\}$$

For there is no difference between Jew and Gentile—the same Lord is Lord of all and richly blesses all who call on him,

Romans 10:12 KJV

MAY 31

Help is on the way. Look over your
shoulder – help is coming up behind
you. Help is coming from an
unexpected place. Expect the
unexpected!

I will lift up mine eyes unto the hills, from whence
cometh my help.

Psalm 121:1 KJV

JUNE 1

{
TGIF
Trusting God In Faith
}

It is better to trust in the Lord than to put confidence in man.

Psalm 118:8 KJV

JUNE 2

(
Good morning
…joy is coming.
)

You make known to me the path of life; you will fill
me with joy in your presence, with eternal pleasures
at your right hand.

Psalm 16:11 NIV

JUNE 3

Today is a good day to celebrate
because after all you've been
through you're still here.

And they overcame him by the blood of the Lamb,
and by the word of their testimony.

Revelation 12:11 KJV

[155]

JUNE 4

> Stop talking about how you feel and
> start confessing what you believe!

We having the same spirit of faith, according as it is
written, I believed, and therefore have I spoken; we
also believe, and therefore speak;

2 Corinthians 4:13 KJV

[156]

JUNE 5

> God will call you out of something
> to lead you into something much
> greater. Acknowledge Him and He
> will direct your path!

He brought me out into a spacious place; he rescued
me because he delighted in me.

Psalm 18:19 NIV

JUNE 6

$$\left[\ \text{True greatness cannot be hidden.}\ \right]$$

Let your light so shine before men, that they may see your good works, and glorify your Father which is in heaven.

Matthew 5:16 KJV

JUNE 7

$$\left(\begin{array}{c} \text{God doesn't need permission to step} \\ \text{into your situation.} \end{array}\right)$$

And when he was come into the temple, the chief priests and the elders of the people came unto him as he was teaching, and said, By what authority doest thou these things? and who gave thee this authority? And Jesus answered and said unto them, I also will ask you one thing, which if ye tell me, I in like wise will tell you by what authority I do these things.

Matthew 21:23 – 24 KJV

JUNE 8

God will give you blessings to keep
your head up and burdens to keep
your knees bent.
Stay prayerful!

Confess your faults one to another, and pray one for another, that ye may be healed. The effectual fervent prayer of a righteous man availeth much.

James 5:16 KJV

JUNE 9

We should help others do what is
right and build them up
in the Lord.
Serve Him.

Let every one of us please his neighbour for his
good to edification.

Romans 15:2 NLT

JUNE 10

> You have been given freedom; not freedom to do wrong, but freedom to love and serve each other.

For, brethren, ye have been called unto liberty; only use not liberty for an occasion to the flesh, but by love serve one another.

Galatians 5:13 KJV

JUNE 11

> You are never alone or without a friend because Jesus says, "Now you are my friend."

Henceforth I call you not servants; for the servant knoweth not what his lord doeth: but I have called you friends; for all things that I have heard of my Father I have made known unto you.

John 15:15 KJV

[163]

JUNE 12

Life has many unanswered
questions. But, one thing is for sure,
true wisdom is found in God, and
true happiness comes from pleasing
Him!

Just as you cannot understand the path of the wind
or the mystery of a tiny baby growing in its
mother's womb, so you cannot understand the
activity of God, who does all things.

Ecclesiastes 11:5 NLT

JUNE 13

You're stronger than you think.
Often times, things come against
you in life in order to show you just
how strong you really are. Samson
had no idea how strong he was until
a lion came against him. You're
stronger than you think!

That he would grant you, according to the riches of
his glory, to be strengthened with might by his
Spirit in the inner man;

Ephesians 3:16 KJV

JUNE 14

JESUS paid the ultimate price and made the ultimate sacrifice for our freedom. Because of Jesus we are now free in our mind, body, and spirit. JESUS HAS MADE US FREE. And those whom the Son has set free, are free indeed! Thank you Lord Jesus for freedom!!

For the law of the Spirit of life in Christ Jesus hath made me free from the law of sin and death.

Romans 8:2 KJV

JUNE 15

We can make our plans, but the final
outcome is in God's hands. Commit
to the Lord whatever you do, and
your plans will succeed.

The preparations of the heart in man, and the
answer of the tongue, is from the LORD.
Commit thy works unto the LORD, and thy thoughts
shall be established.

Proverbs 16:1, 3 KJV

JUNE 16

Forget those things that have kept you hindered in the past, and keep on pressing for your blessing. You can win!

Brethren, I count not myself to have apprehended: but this one thing I do, forgetting those things which are behind, and reaching forth unto those things which are before, I press toward the mark for the prize of the high calling of God in Christ Jesus.

Philippians 3:13 – 14 KJV

JUNE 17

Don't dwell on your past, it's
already gone. Instead, focus on the
relationship you have with God in
the here and now. Understand, you
have been forgiven for your past!

Brethren, I count not myself to have apprehended:
but this one thing I do, forgetting those things which
are behind, and reaching forth unto those things
which are before,

Philippians 3:13a KJV

JUNE 18

When you have nothing else to lose,
you have everything to gain. So roll
up your sleeves and go for it! Don't
give up! Don't Quit!

And there were four leprous men at the entering in
of the gate: and they said one to another, Why sit
we here until we die? If we say, We will enter into
the city, then the famine is in the city, and we shall
die there: and if we sit still here, we die also. Now
therefore come, and let us fall unto the host of the
Syrians: if they save us alive, we shall live; and if
they kill us, we shall but die.

2 Kings 7:3 – 4 KJV

JUNE 19

There is no need to fear because
your Heavenly Father is always
near. Thank Him for His presence!
Be of good courage!

For I am the Lord your God who takes hold of your
right hand and says to you, Do not fear; I will help
you.

Isaiah 41:13 NIV

JUNE 20

God has given you the keys of the
Kingdom. Now, what doors are you
opening in your life, or better yet,
what doors are you closing?
Authority, dominion, and
Power – are in your hands!

And I will give unto thee the keys of the kingdom
of heaven: and whatsoever thou shalt bind on earth
shall be bound in heaven: and whatsoever thou shalt
loose on earth shall be loosed in heaven.

Matthew 16:19 KJV

JUNE 21

> God's word is not just idle words for
> you ; they are life. Nourish yourself
> in His word and your faith
> will grow strong!

For the word of God is alive and active. Sharper than any double-edged sword, it penetrates even to dividing soul and spirit, joints and marrow; it judges the thoughts and attitudes of the heart.

Hebrews 4:12 KJV

JUNE 22

Christ has freed us from disappointment, discouragement, and the prison of the past. Don't allow anyone or anything to cause you to return to bondage. Walk in the fullness of your freedom!

Stand fast therefore in the liberty wherewith Christ hath made us free, and be not entangled again with the yoke of bondage.

Galatians 5:1 KJV

JUNE 23

Today is a good day because your
victory, your healing, your joy, your
peace, your freedom, and your
inheritance was won by God's only
begotten Son! Glory Hallelujah!
Thank You, Lord!

But thanks be to God! He gives us the victory
through our Lord Jesus Christ.

1 Corinthians 15:57 NIV

JUNE 24

[
Jesus did it just for me!
]

Who, being in the form of God, thought it not robbery to be equal with God: But made himself of no reputation, and took upon him the form of a servant, and was made in the likeness of men:

Philippians 2:6 – 7 KJV

JUNE 25

> Give God some praise today because He was broken and beaten so you can be whole, and whipped so you can be healed.

But he was wounded for our transgressions, he was bruised for our iniquities: the chastisement of our peace was upon him; and with his stripes we are healed.

Isaiah 53:5 KJV

JUNE 26

> When obedient, you and your family
> shall rejoice in everything you have
> put your hand to; because the Lord
> has blessed you!
> Obedience is better!

And there ye shall eat before the LORD your God, and ye shall rejoice in all that ye put your hand unto, ye and your households, wherein the LORD thy God hath blessed thee.

Deuteronomy 12:7 KJV

JUNE 27

{
Struggles are often the enemy distracting you from what God is really doing in your life. Stay focused. God is working in you!
}

For we wrestle not against flesh and blood, but against principalities, against powers, against the rulers of the darkness of this world, against spiritual wickedness in high places.

Ephesians 6:12 KJV

JUNE 28

DECLARE THIS:
"I will not be afraid because the
Lord is with me. People can't do
anything to me."

The LORD is on my side; I will not fear: what can
man do unto me?

Psalm 118:6 KJV

JUNE 29

> Today is a good day because you have been chosen! The Lord has chosen you to be His treasured possession. God loves you!

For thou art an holy people unto the LORD thy God, and the LORD hath chosen thee to be a peculiar people unto himself, above all the nations that are upon the earth.

Deuteronomy 14:2 KJV

JUNE 30

{
When your situation seems
hopeless, determine that no matter
how bad things become you will
continue to pray. Don't turn away
from your most faithful friend.
}

But I keep praying to you, Lord, hoping this time
you will show me favor. In your unfailing love, O
God, answer my prayer with your sure salvation.

Psalm 69:13 NLT

JULY 1

Our God is an awesome God! He gives power and strength to His people. Receive it today!

O God, thou art terrible out of thy holy places: the God of Israel is he that giveth strength and power unto his people. Blessed be God.

Psalm 68:35 KJV

JULY 2

> Don't hold on to your burdens – give them to the One who carries them on a daily basis!

For my yoke is easy, and my burden is light.

Matthew 11:30 KJV

JULY 3

The way to overcome doubt and
insecurity is by…Action!

Arise therefore, and get thee down, and go with
them, doubting nothing: for I have sent them.

Acts 10:20 KJV

JULY 4

No matter how challenging this day
may be, you will have the strength
to meet every challenge!
Be Strong!

Thy shoes shall be iron and brass; and as thy days,
so shall thy strength be.

Deuteronomy 33:25 KJV

JULY 5

$$\left(\begin{array}{c} \text{God's plan for me is perfect;} \\ \text{sometimes the problem is user error!} \end{array} \right)$$

The instructions of the Lord are perfect, reviving the soul.

Psalm 19:7 NLT

JULY 6

> Praise be to God, who has not rejected your prayers or withheld His love from you!

Praise be to God, who has not rejected my prayer or withheld his love from me!

Psalm 66:20 NIV

JULY 7

$$\left\{ \begin{array}{c} \text{Shout with joy to God! Sing the} \\ \text{glory of His name; make His praise} \\ \text{glorious.} \end{array} \right\}$$

Make a joyful noise unto God, all ye lands:
Sing forth the honour of his name: make his praise
glorious.

Psalm 66:1 – 2 KJV

JULY 8

God's endless provision will supply
your need! Trust Him! Provision
means "a providing beforehand." In
other words, God knows your story
and He made arrangements to care
for you long before you needed it.

For the jar of flour was not used up and the jug of
oil did not run dry, in keeping with the word of the
Lord spoken by Elijah.

1 Kings 17:16 NIV

JULY 9

Victory belongs to YOU because YOU belong to GOD! Victory in Jesus!

Now this I know: The Lord gives victory to his anointed. He answers him from his heavenly sanctuary with the victorious power of his right hand.

Psalm 20:6 NIV

JULY 10

{
DECLARE THIS:
"Today I exercise diligence, for the
hand of the diligent maketh rich!"
}

He becometh poor that dealeth with a slack hand:
but the hand of the diligent maketh rich.

Proverbs 10:4 KJV

JULY 11

Today is a good day because God
has you covered by His grace!
Be Blessed!

But unto every one of us is given grace according to
the measure of the gift of Christ.

Ephesians 4:7 KJV

JULY 12

Dare to trust God. He has never
failed before, and the good news is,
He is not about to start now. Have
faith.

The grass withereth, the flower fadeth: but the word
of our God shall stand for ever.

Isaiah 40:8 KJV

JULY 13

It takes faith to identify the
difference between counterfeit
blessings and the blessings of the
Lord.

The blessing of the LORD brings wealth, without
painful toil for it.

Proverbs 10:22 NIV

JULY 14

You need a good balance of
physical and spiritual exercise in
order to be at your best for God's
service. Exercise often and pray
more often!

Beloved, I wish above all things that thou mayest
prosper and be in health, even as thy soul
prospereth.

3 John 2 KJV

JULY 15

> The enemy tempts us to take things
> from us, but God tests us to get
> things to us!
> Obedience is better than sacrifice.

He gave you manna to eat in the wilderness,
something your ancestors had never known, to
humble and test you so that in the end it might go
well with you.

Deuteronomy 8:16 NIV

JULY 16

If storms are raging in your life,
remember who is in the storm with
you; Jesus, the One who can calm
the storm.

Be still, and know that I am God: I will be exalted
among the heathen, I will be exalted in the earth.

Psalm 46:10 KJV

JULY 17

DECLARE THIS:
"This day, I do all things to the Glory of God, and am fruitful in every good work!" Have a blessed day!

That ye might walk worthy of the Lord unto all pleasing, being fruitful in every good work, and increasing in the knowledge of God;

Colossians 1:10 KJV

JULY 18

[Dare to believe!]

Jesus said unto him, If thou canst believe, all things are possible to him that believeth.

Mark 9:23 KJV

JULY 19

Start expecting unprecedented favor.
Believe that God will do something
extraordinary in your life!

"...and that the time of the LORD's favor has come."

Luke 4:19 NLT

JULY 20

It is natural to share a good bargain
with others, so it should also be
natural to share what God has done
for you. Let the redeemed of the
Lord say so!

I have told all your people about your justice. I have
not been afraid to speak out, as you, O Lord, well
know.

Psalm 40:9 NLT

JULY 21

"Yes, Lord!" When you put a "Yes, Lord" in your spirit, yes places you in His face - Lord places you at His feet! Put a "Yes, Lord" in your spirit!

God is a Spirit: and they that worship him must worship him in spirit and in truth.

John 4:24 KJV

JULY 22

Don't hold back. Don't be timid. Be strong! Be confident because God will place all your enemies under your feet when you fight them.

And it came to pass, when they brought out those kings unto Joshua, that Joshua called for all the men of Israel, and said unto the captains of the men of war which went with him, Come near, put your feet upon the necks of these kings. And they came near, and put their feet upon the necks of them. And Joshua said unto them, Fear not, nor be dismayed, be strong and of good courage: for thus shall the LORD do to all your enemies against whom ye fight.

Joshua 10:24 – 25 KJV

[204]

JULY 23

Rest in God's love because He loved
you even in your darkest moments!

But God commendeth his love toward us, in that,
while we were yet sinners, Christ died for us.

Romans 5:8 KJV

JULY 24

$$\left(\begin{array}{c} \text{DECLARE THIS:} \\ \text{"I will greatly rejoice in the Lord;} \\ \text{my soul shall be joyful in my God."} \\ \text{Be joyful!} \end{array} \right)$$

I will greatly rejoice in the LORD, my soul shall be joyful in my God; for he hath clothed me with the garments of salvation, he hath covered me with the robe of righteousness, as a bridegroom decketh himself with ornaments, and as a bride adorneth herself with her jewels.

Isaiah 61:10 KJV

JULY 25

> The joy of the Lord is your strength, so don't allow negative people to steal your joy. When you lose your joy, you lose your strength!

Then he said unto them, Go your way, eat the fat, and drink the sweet, and send portions unto them for whom nothing is prepared: for this day is holy unto our Lord: neither be ye sorry; for the joy of the Lord is your strength.

Nehemiah 8:10 KJV

JULY 26

Be glad in knowing that ultimate joy comes from Christ dwelling within you. He who lives within you will fulfill His purposes for you!

Rejoice in the Lord always: and again I say, Rejoice.

Philippians 4:4 KJV

JULY 27

Don't give up!

You need to persevere so that when you have done the will of God, you will receive what he has promised.

Hebrews 10:36 NIV

JULY 28

Whatever you're going through,
remember God is working
everything together for your good.
Be blessed. No worries!

Rather, worship the Lord your God; it is he who
will deliver you from the hand of all your enemies."

2 Kings 17:39 NIV

JULY 29

> Regardless of the circumstances –
> you were created by God, which
> makes you valuable. You may not
> be able to provide everything they
> want, but you are supplying
> everything they need, which is
> YOU!

For you created my inmost being; you knit me
together in my mother's womb.

Psalm 139:13 NIV

JULY 30

You're not going to bankrupt God
by asking for abundant blessings. He
is the God of more than enough.
Increase your faith!

The Lord shall increase you more and more, you
and your children.

Psalm 115:14 KJV

JULY 31

$$\left[\text{Knowing God produces great things!} \right]$$

but the people that do know their God shall be strong, and do exploits.

Daniel 11:32b KJV

AUGUST 1

We serve a "BIG" God, so stop thinking so small - spread out and dream bigger. Lord, enlarge my territory!

Enlarge the place of your tent, stretch your tent curtains wide, do not hold back; lengthen your cords, strengthen your stakes.

Isaiah 54:2 NIV

AUGUST 2

> You have authority over your
> circumstances – your circumstances
> don't have authority over you!

Thou madest him to have dominion over the works
of thy hands; thou hast put all things under his feet:

Psalm 8:6 KJV

AUGUST 3

$$\Big[\quad \text{Standing on the promises!} \quad \Big]$$

My eyes stay open through the watches of the night,
that I may meditate on your promises.

Psalm 119:148 NIV

AUGUST 4

Whatever you're going through –
God arms you with strength for the
battle. Be strengthened!

You armed me with strength for battle; you
humbled my adversaries before me.

Psalm 18:39 NIV

AUGUST 5

{
The measure of success is how you
deal with disappointment and
setbacks. Persevere!
}

These things I have spoken unto you, that in me ye
might have peace. In the world ye shall have
tribulation: but be of good cheer; I have overcome
the world.

John 16:33 KJV

AUGUST 6

You have been chosen for greatness!
Greatness awaits!

And I will make of thee a great nation, and I will bless thee, and make thy name great; and thou shalt be a blessing:

Genesis 12:2 KJV

AUGUST 7

Lighten up your life. Stop living in
the dark!

I am come a light into the world, that whosoever
believeth on me should not abide in darkness.

John 12:46 KJV

AUGUST 8

$$\left(\quad \text{Are you prepared for what God has prepared for you?} \quad \right)$$

But as it is written, Eye hath not seen, nor ear heard, neither have entered into the heart of man, the things which God hath prepared for them that love him.

1 Corinthians 2:9 KJV

AUGUST 9

> God has made many promises. They
> are all "Yes" because of what Christ
> has done. So through Christ we say,
> "Amen." We want God to receive
> glory.

The Lord is trustworthy in all he promises and
faithful in all he does.

Psalm 145:13 NIV

AUGUST 10

(
DECLARE THIS:
"I will overcome every obstacle,
defeat every enemy, and become
everything God has created me to
be!"
Be empowered!
)

But you give us victory over our enemies, you put
our adversaries to shame.

Psalm 44:7 NIV

AUGUST 11

[Better things are coming!]

Verily, verily, I say unto you, He that believeth on me, the works that I do shall he do also; and greater works than these shall he do; because I go unto my Father.

John 14:12 KJV

AUGUST 12

> Regardless of the circumstances, if
> you demonstrate great faith in God –
> God will demonstrate great miracles
> in you!

Then Jesus answered and said unto her, O woman,
great is thy faith: be it unto thee even as thou wilt.
And her daughter was made whole from that very
hour.

Matthew 15:28 KJV

AUGUST 13

Every place where your faith and courage lead you to go, shall be yours. Your inheritance shall have no limits, but those set by your own unbelief and fears. As far as you will tread, you shall possess! Possess it! Go get it! It's yours!

So on that day Moses swore to me, 'The land on which your feet have walked will be your inheritance and that of your children forever, because you have followed the Lord my God wholeheartedly.

Joshua 14:9 KJV

AUGUST 14

There may be a daunting task before
you, but remember you are not in
this alone. You can do all things
through Christ!

Have not I commanded thee? Be strong and of a
good courage; be not afraid, neither be thou
dismayed: for the LORD thy God is with thee
whithersoever thou goest.

Joshua 1:9 KJV

AUGUST 15

Each day you face tough situations, difficult people, and temptations. God promises to never abandon you or fail to help you. You can conquer life's challenges with God's direction.

No one will be able to stand against you as long as you live. For I will be with you as I was with Moses. I will not fail you or abandon you.

Joshua 1:5 NLT

AUGUST 16

$$\Big[\ \text{Today, I choose joy!}\ \Big]$$

Be joyful in hope, patient in affliction, faithful in prayer.

Romans 12:12 NIV

AUGUST 17

Take back EVERYTHING that the enemy has stolen from you – your joy, your peace, your happiness. Take it back! Kingdom Authority!

And from the days of John the Baptist until now the kingdom of heaven suffereth violence, and the violent take it by force.

Matthew 11:12 KJV

AUGUST 18

Get ready! God is saying it's going
to happen sooner than you think.
You're coming into acceleration.
Buckle up! Take the brakes off!

He sends his command to the earth; his word runs
swiftly.

Psalm 147:15 NIV

AUGUST 19

Whatever God has predestined for your life Jesus says, "Let it be so now." The healing that God has for your life – let it be so now. The business idea that God has given you – let it be so now. The ministry that God has given you – let it be so now. The marriage that God has for you – let it be so now. Whatever God has placed on your heart to do for the kingdom – let it be so…NOW!

Jesus replied, "Let it be so now; it is proper for us to do this to fulfill all righteousness."

Matthew 3:15a NIV

AUGUST 20

It doesn't matter what your boss
says; what the doctor says; what
your bank account says; what the
government says; what your friends
say or what the haters say, when
JESUS says, "Yes!" – NOBODY
can say no!

Jesus looked at them and said, "With man this is
impossible, but with God all things are possible."

Matthew 19:26 NIV

AUGUST 21

Get ready for the explosion that will take place in your life. Explosion is defined as a sudden, widespread increase. There will be a sudden, widespread increase in your life when your faith – and – your miracle collides with reality!
BOOM!

I have declared the former things from the beginning; and they went forth out of my mouth, and I shewed them; I did them suddenly, and they came to pass.

Isaiah 48:3 KJV

AUGUST 22

> The gift that keeps on giving is available to all who will receive Him. Jesus Christ was born so we can be born again!

For unto you is born this day in the city of David a Saviour, which is Christ the Lord.
Glory to God in the highest, and on earth peace, good will toward men.

Luke 2:11, 14 KJV

AUGUST 23

$\left\{\begin{array}{c}\text{The LORD will fulfill his purpose}\\\text{for you. God had a purpose in mind}\\\text{when you were born and He will}\\\text{fulfill that purpose!}\end{array}\right\}$

The LORD will   vindicate me;   your   love, LORD, endures forever— do not abandon the works of your hands.

Psalm 138:8 NIV

AUGUST 24

Optimism is a lifestyle not a way of thinking. This day, choose to be positive and don't allow negative people or circumstances to steal your joy.

Be glad in the LORD, and rejoice, ye righteous: and shout for joy, all ye that are upright in heart.

Psalm 32:11 KJV

AUGUST 25

> The Lord is going to do something
> in your life that you will not believe.
> IS ANYTHING TOO HARD FOR
> GOD!?

Behold, I am the Lord, the God of all flesh: is there
any thing too hard for me?

Jeremiah 32:27 KJV

AUGUST 26

O taste and see that the LORD is good. You've tasted everything else, now give God a chance to show you how good He is. As we trust Him daily, we experience just how good He is. Great blessings are in store for those who trust Him!

O taste and see that the LORD is good: blessed is the man that trusteth in him.

Psalm 34:8 KJV

AUGUST 27

> The same God who showed His
> limitless provision to 5,000 people
> by feeding them, wants to show you
> His limitless power. Expect a
> miracle!

Do you still not understand? Don't you remember
the five loaves for the five thousand, and how many
basketfuls you gathered?

Matthew 16:9 NIV

AUGUST 28

$$\left(\begin{array}{c} \text{Regardless of what you're facing} \\ \text{today, God can do the impossible in} \\ \text{your life.} \end{array}\right)$$

The righteous is delivered out of trouble,

Proverbs 11:8a KJV

AUGUST 29

You thought you weren't going to make it; you thought you would be crushed under the weight of pressure; you thought you were out of strength, but you're stronger than you think. God is about to increase your strength!

He giveth power to the faint; and to them that have no might he increaseth strength.

Isaiah 40:29 KJV

AUGUST 30

Don't allow the clouds in your life to overshadow the sun. You have so much to be thankful for. Let the "Son" shine through in every area of your life!

And he was transfigured before them: and his face did shine as the sun, and his raiment was white as the light.

Matthew 17:2 KJV

AUGUST 31

You may or may not have been paid
today, but one thing is for sure -
Jesus paid it all for you. You never
have to worry about paying this bill
because your account has been
PAID IN FULL!
Live Free!

In whom we have redemption through his blood,
even the forgiveness of sins.

Colossians 1:14 KJV

SEPTEMBER 1

> May you be strengthened with all his glorious power so you will have all the endurance and patience you need.

Be strong and courageous. Do not be afraid or terrified because of them, for the Lord your God goes with you; he will never leave you nor forsake you.

Deuteronomy 31:6 NIV

SEPTEMBER 2

> Jesus is Lord over every situation
> and circumstance. Every enemy you
> face must bow its knee to His
> authority. There is nothing that can
> stop His plan for your life. Continue
> to trust Him and He will see you
> through to the other side of your
> situation.

For it is written, As I live, saith the Lord, every knee shall bow to me, and every tongue shall confess to God.

Romans 14:11 KJV

SEPTEMBER 3

That which you have been believing
God for is already done...now just
wait for your change to come!

Wait on the Lord: be of good courage, and he shall
strengthen thine heart: wait, I say, on the Lord.

Psalm 27:14 KJV

SEPTEMBER 4

Your best days are not behind you –
your best days are ahead of you.
God has so much more in store for
your life. It's not over, it's only the
beginning. Your future will be
greater than your past; Let go of the
past and reach toward the bright
future that God has planned for
your life!

...old things are passed away; behold, all things are
become new.

2 Corinthians 5:17b KJV

SEPTEMBER 5

God loves you! God loves you so much that He sent His one and only Son to die for you. Not because you were good enough, but just because He loved you. For God to give up so much for you; there is no way He would leave you in your time of need. God's love will cover you and help you to meet every challenge and trial that you face.

For God so loved the world, that he gave his only begotten Son, that whosoever believeth in him should not perish, but have everlasting life.

John 3:16 KJV

SEPTEMBER 6

You walk in victory because you
are a child of God, and faith is what
gives you the victory.
DECLARE THIS:
"I will overcome every obstacle,
defeat every enemy, and become
everything God has created me to
be; because I walk in victory as a
child of God!"

For everyone born of God overcomes the world.
This is the victory that has overcome the world,
even our faith.

1 John 5:4 NIV

SEPTEMBER 7

The Lord will keep you from all harm; He will watch over your life.

The LORD shall preserve thee from all evil: he shall preserve thy soul.

Psalm 121:7 KJV

SEPTEMBER 8

{
This day belongs to the Lord! Let's celebrate and be glad today.
}

I was glad when they said unto me, Let us go into the house of the Lord.

Psalm 122:1 KJV

SEPTEMBER 9

If you find life difficult because
you're doing what God said, take it
in stride. Trust Him. He knows what
He's doing and He'll keep on doing
it.

Wherefore let them that suffer according to the will
of God commit the keeping of their souls to him in
well doing, as unto a faithful Creator.

1 Peter 4:19 KJV

[253]

SEPTEMBER 10

I'm thankful for life, health, and strength. What are you thankful for?

Enter into his gates with thanksgiving, and into his courts with praise: be thankful unto him, and bless his name.

Psalm 100:4 KJV

SEPTEMBER 11

{ You can doubt me, but don't doubt my God; He's too big. }

But will God really live on earth? Why, even the highest heavens cannot contain you. How much less this Temple I have built!

1 Kings 8:27 NLT

SEPTEMBER 12

$$\left(\begin{array}{c}\text{In the Kingdom of God, it is more}\\\text{important to give justice and mercy}\\\text{than to receive it. By loving and}\\\text{praying for your enemies, you can}\\\text{overcome evil with good.}\end{array}\right)$$

But I say unto you, That ye resist not evil: but whosoever shall smite thee on thy right cheek, turn to him the other also.

Matthew 5:39 KJV

SEPTEMBER 13

When the pressures of life causes
you to worry, fear, or doubt, you
must stand firm on God's word.
DECLARE:
"I will not be afraid, because the
Lord is with me. People can't do
anything to me. The Lord is with
me to help me, so I will see my
enemies defeated."

Devise your strategy, but it will be thwarted;
propose your plan, but it will not stand, for God is
with us.

Isaiah 8:10 NIV

SEPTEMBER 14

$$\left\{ \begin{array}{c} \text{We were not born for just "self" --} \\ \text{we were born for "service."} \end{array} \right\}$$

But you are not to be like that. Instead, the greatest among you should be like the youngest, and the one who rules like the one who serves.

Luke 22:26 NIV

SEPTEMBER 15

You are made complete through your union with Christ. Since the presence of God has taken up residence in your life, you are a new person that is equipped for life. Take advantage of your new life, step outside of the box or the boat – God will guide you. Give more generously – God will supply. Love more freely – God will energize you. Say "can do" more often – God will amaze you!

And ye are complete in him, which is the head of all principality and power:

Colossians 2:10 KJV

SEPTEMBER 16

$$\left(\begin{array}{c} \text{Generosity proves that your heart} \\ \text{has been cleansed of self-serving} \\ \text{and filled with a God serving spirit.} \\ \text{Do people see generosity in your} \\ \text{actions?} \end{array} \right)$$

Because of the service by which you have proved
yourselves, others will praise God for the obedience
that accompanies your confession of the gospel of
Christ, and for your generosity in sharing with them
and with everyone else.

2 Corinthians 9:13 NIV

SEPTEMBER 17

Rid yourself of negative thoughts that occupy your mind. You can recognize negative thoughts and change them or you can allow negative thoughts to take you captive.

Casting down imaginations, and every high thing that exalteth itself against the knowledge of God, and bringing into captivity every thought to the obedience of Christ.

2 Corinthians 10:5 KJV

SEPTEMBER 18

Time is so precious. Once it passes, you can't get it back. Don't waste your precious time on anyone or anything that is not contributing to you reaching your destiny or purpose in life. You can't afford to waste time because you have somewhere to go! Tick, tock, tick, tock....

To every thing there is a season, and a time to every purpose under the heaven:

Ecclesiastes 3:1 KJV

SEPTEMBER 19

$$\Bigg(\quad\begin{array}{c}\text{The effectiveness of your time spent}\\\text{with God can be measured by the}\\\text{effect it has on your behavior and}\\\text{attitude. Do you put into action what}\\\text{you hear?}\end{array}\quad\Bigg)$$

But don't just listen to God's word. You must do what it says. Otherwise, you are only fooling yourselves.

James 1:22 NLT

SEPTEMBER 20

> With God all things are possible, so
> dwell in the possibilities. He can do
> exceedingly and abundantly above
> all you can ask or think. Continue to
> trust Him, and you will see the
> impossible become possible in your
> life. Live a life of limitless
> possibilities!

Let the morning bring me word of your unfailing
love, for I have put my trust in you. Show me the
way I should go, for to you I entrust my life.

Psalm 143:8 NIV

SEPTEMBER 21

God will never allow difficult times to overwhelm you. He will always be there to see you through to the other side of trouble. Hold on - God will make everything alright!

My brethren, count it all joy when ye fall into divers temptations; Knowing this, that the trying of your faith worketh patience. But let patience have her perfect work, that ye may be perfect and entire, wanting nothing.

James 1:2 – 4 KJV

SEPTEMBER 22

May the God of peace equip you
with all you need for doing His will.
May He produce in you, through the
power of Jesus Christ, every good
thing that is pleasing to Him.

Now the God of peace, that brought again from the
dead our Lord Jesus, that great shepherd of the
sheep, through the blood of the everlasting
covenant, Make you perfect in every good work to
do his will, working in you that which is
wellpleasing in his sight, through Jesus Christ; to
whom be glory for ever and ever. Amen.

Hebrews 13:20 – 21 KJV

SEPTEMBER 23

> Let us run with endurance the race
> God has set before us. We do this
> by keeping our eyes on Jesus, the
> champion who initiates and perfects
> our faith. There is a champion
> within you. Let Him guide you to
> the victory that was preordained for
> your life!

Wherefore seeing we also are compassed about with so great a cloud of witnesses, let us lay aside every weight, and the sin which doth so easily beset us, and let us run with patience the race that is set before us, Looking unto Jesus the author and finisher of our faith; who for the joy that was set before him endured the cross, despising the shame, and is set down at the right hand of the throne of God.

Hebrews 12: 1 – 2 KJV

SEPTEMBER 24

God not only has a plan for your
life, but He also has a plan for the
lives of your children. Pray, protect,
and prepare them to do the work
God has planned for them to do.
Faith allows us to entrust even our
children to God. God's about to do
something in the lives of your
children because of your
faithfulness!

By faith Moses, when he was born, was hid three
months of his parents, because they saw he was a
proper child; and they were not afraid of the king's
commandment.

Hebrews 11:23 KJV

SEPTEMBER 25

You demonstrate true faith when
you believe God will fulfill His
promises (even though you don't see
those promises materializing yet).
Hold on to your faith!

Now faith is the substance of things hoped for, the
evidence of things not seen.

Hebrews 11:1 KJV

SEPTEMBER 26

Don't lose your confidence. It will bring you a great reward. You need endurance so that after you have done what God wants you to do, you can receive what He has promised. We don't belong with those who turn back and are destroyed. Instead, we belong with those who have faith and are saved.

Cast not away therefore your confidence, which hath great recompence of reward. For ye have need of patience, that, after ye have done the will of God, ye might receive the promise.
But we are not of them who draw back unto perdition; but of them that believe to the saving of the soul.

Hebrews 10:35 – 36, 39 KJV

SEPTEMBER 27

When you fall into deep trouble, it is
best to fall into the hands of the
Lord – instead of the hands of
people. The Lord has mercy; people
have malice.

The faithful love of the LORD never ends! His
mercies never cease.

Lamentations 3:22 ESV

SEPTEMBER 28

$$\left\{ \begin{array}{c} \text{God will protect you by guiding you} \\ \text{through painful circumstances, not} \\ \text{only by helping you to escape them.} \end{array} \right\}$$

But the salvation of the righteous is of the LORD: he is their strength in the time of trouble.

Psalm 37:39 KJV

SEPTEMBER 29

The secret to your promise is revealed in your worship. When you share your admiration with God, He shares His secrets with you. Make sure to spend some time with Him today!

Give unto the Lord the glory due unto his name; worship the Lord in the beauty of holiness. Make sure to spend some time with Him today!

Psalm 29:2 KJV

SEPTEMBER 30

{
There is a lost world waiting for you
to overcome "what was done to
you." It's time to let it go and be
free!
}

"Even if they sin against you seven times in a day
and seven times come back to you saying 'I repent,'
you must forgive them."

Luke 17:4 KJV

OCTOBER 1

Your hard work; your persistence;
your diligence will not be in vain.
Like a laborious farmer, your
harvest is on the way!

...but the hand of the diligent maketh rich.

Proverbs 10:4b KJV

OCTOBER 2

God is the robed and ruling King. Everything that you face that is not of God is subject to the power of the Lord's reign. So, give your problems to the One who can rule in your favor!

The LORD reigns, he is robed in majesty; the LORD is robed in majesty and armed with strength; indeed, the world is established, firm and secure.

Psalm 93:1 KJV

OCTOBER 3

The forecast for today is THE LORD REIGNS. No need for an umbrella because HE reigns with power and majesty. Regardless of the situations that you may face today, the Lord reigns high above them all, and has the power to turn them around. It's going to work in your favor!

Yours, Lord, is the greatness and the power and the glory and the majesty and the splendor, for everything in heaven and earth is yours. Yours, Lord, is the kingdom; you are exalted as head over all.

1 Chronicles 29:11 NIV

OCTOBER 4

$$\left\{\begin{array}{c} \text{May God's best and the greatest of} \\ \text{the Kingdom be yours as we possess} \\ \text{the land; Go get it} - \text{it's yours!} \end{array}\right\}$$

Therefore, since we are receiving a kingdom that cannot be shaken, let us be thankful, and so worship God acceptably with reverence and awe.

Hebrews 12:28 KJV

OCTOBER 5

People will make weapons to fight against you, but their weapons will not defeat you. Some people will say things against you, but anyone who speaks against you will be proved wrong.

These benefits are enjoyed by the servants of the Lord; their vindication will come from me. I, the Lord, have spoken!

Isaiah 54:17 NLT

OCTOBER 6

When you feel that God has forgotten you in your troubles, remember that God has a schedule that you can't see. God knows the best time to act!

God heard their groaning and he remembered his covenant with Abraham, with Isaac and with Jacob. So God looked on the Israelites and was concerned about them.

Exodus 2:24 – 25 KJV

OCTOBER 7

$\left\{\begin{array}{c}\end{array}\right.$ God is in control no matter what happens. We may not know what the future holds but we do know Who holds the future. Trust Him! $\left.\begin{array}{c}\end{array}\right\}$

My own hand laid the foundations of the earth, and my right hand spread out the heavens; when I summon them, they all stand up together.

Isaiah 48:13 KJV

OCTOBER 8

Your footsteps are ordered by the Lord, which means nothing or no one can prevent you from reaching your destiny.

A man's heart deviseth his way: but the Lord directeth his steps.

Proverbs 16:9 KJV

OCTOBER 9

{ God is faithful. He will trouble those who trouble you, and give relief to those who are troubled. }

For in the time of trouble he shall hide me in his pavilion:

Psalm 27:5a KJV

OCTOBER 10

$$\left\{ \begin{array}{c} \text{May God give you the power to} \\ \text{accomplish all the good things your} \\ \text{faith prompts you to do.} \end{array} \right\}$$

But ye shall receive power, after that the Holy Ghost is come upon you:

Acts 1:8a KJV

OCTOBER 11

I pray that by His power God will make every good thing you have planned come true. I pray that He will make perfect all that you have done by faith. Stretch your faith – reach higher – God will do it for you…if you trust Him!

Wherefore also we pray always for you, that our God would count you worthy of this calling, and fulfil all the good pleasure of his goodness, and the work of faith with power:

2 Thessalonians 1:11 KJV

OCTOBER 12

$\Big\{$ I speak, "PEACE BE STILL" to every stormy situation that you may face today. $\Big\}$

And he arose, and rebuked the wind, and said unto the sea, Peace, be still.

Mark 4:39 KJV

OCTOBER 13

$$\left(\begin{array}{c} \text{God has heard your prayers and} \\ \text{He's working on a solution to your} \\ \text{situation.} \end{array} \right)$$

For the eyes of the Lord are over the righteous, and his ears are open unto their prayers:

1 Peter 3:12a KJV

OCTOBER 14

We should not thank God "for" everything that happens to us, but "in" everything. We should not thank God "for" the calamity that shows up on our doorstep, but we should thank God for His presence "in" the midst of the calamity when it comes through the door.

I will bow down toward your holy temple and will praise your name for your unfailing love and your faithfulness, for you have so exalted your solemn decree that it surpasses your fame. When I called, you answered me; you greatly emboldened me.

Psalm 138:2 – 3 KJV

OCTOBER 15

> Don't think negatively of the work
> that you do on your job each and
> every day. Instead, consider the
> work that you do as an act of
> worship or a service to the Lord.
> Having this view would remove
> some of the struggle and boredom
> out of it. We can work free of anger
> and resentment if we treat some of
> the issues we face on the job as the
> cost of discipleship.

They traded the truth about God for a lie. So they
worshiped and served the things God created
instead of the Creator himself, who is worthy of
eternal praise!

Romans 1:25 KJV

OCTOBER 16

⎧ Are you properly dressed today? ⎫

Therefore, as God's chosen people, holy and dearly loved, clothe yourselves with compassion, kindness, humility, gentleness and patience.

Colossians 3:12 NIV

OCTOBER 17

Don't give up on God because He won't give up on you. Hold on...God will do it for you!

Beareth all things, believeth all things, hopeth all things, endureth all things.

1 Corinthians 13:7 KJV

OCTOBER 18

Don't worry about anything but pray about everything. Worry brings sleepless nights, but prayer brings peaceful days.

Do not be anxious about anything, but in every situation, by prayer and petition, with thanksgiving, present your requests to God.

Philippians 4:6 NIV

OCTOBER 19

Give thanks to the Lord, proclaim
his greatness! Let the world know
what He has done. What are you
thankful for?

O give thanks unto the LORD; call upon his name:
make known his deeds among the people.

Psalm 105:1 KJV

OCTOBER 20

Prayer is the key that unlocks faith in your life. Effective prayer needs both the attitude of dependence and the action of asking. Prayer changes things!

Jesus replied, "This kind can be cast out only by prayer.

Mark 9:29 NLT

OCTOBER 21

$\left[\right.$ Rejoice in the Lord today! $\left.\right]$

Glory in his holy name; let the hearts of those who seek the Lord rejoice.

1 Chronicles 16:10 KJV

OCTOBER 22

You have been forgiven; now extend
some forgiveness to others. Don't
give the enemy an opportunity to
divide us.

Neither give place to the devil.

Ephesians 4:27 KJV

OCTOBER 23

Give God a sacrifice of thankfulness today. Only you know just how much He has done for you. Tell Him, "Thank you!"

Let them offer sacrifices of thanksgiving and sing joyfully about his glorious acts.

Psalm 107:22 NLT

[297]

OCTOBER 24

God will open doors for you as you
walk in obedience towards what He
has predestined for your life!

Obedience is better than sacrifice,

1 Samuel 15:22c NLT

OCTOBER 25

I speak, "Life!" to every area of your
life that the enemy has tried to
destroy!

The soothing tongue is a tree of life,

Proverbs 15:4a NIV

OCTOBER 26

{
I DECLARE:
"Wisdom, strength, courage, peace,
and prosperity be multiplied in your
life."
}

Grace and peace be yours in abundance through the knowledge of God and of Jesus our Lord.

2 Peter 1:2 NIV

OCTOBER 27

$$\left[\begin{array}{c} \text{This is the last day of your "weak."} \\ \text{Be strong and courageous!} \end{array} \right]$$

Therefore I take pleasure in infirmities, in reproaches, in necessities, in persecutions, in distresses for Christ's sake: for when I am weak, then am I strong.

2 Corinthians 12:10 KJV

OCTOBER 28

Stop living below your standard. You are a child of God. And since you are His child, God guarantees an inheritance is waiting for you.

Wherefore thou art no more a servant, but a son; and if a son, then an heir of God through Christ.

Galatians 4:7 KJV

OCTOBER 29

$$\left\{ \quad \text{Hold on – Victory is coming!} \quad \right\}$$

With God we will gain the victory, and he will trample down our enemies.

Psalm 60:12 NIV

OCTOBER 30

$$\left\{ \begin{array}{c} \text{I pray that God will shower you with} \\ \text{His voluntary and loving FAVOR as} \\ \text{you come to Him today.} \end{array} \right\}$$

May the grace of the Lord Jesus Christ, and the love of God, and the fellowship of the Holy Spirit be with you all.

2 Corinthians 13:14 NIV

OCTOBER 31

{ GOD'S WEIGHT LOSS PLAN: }

Cast your burden on the Lord [releasing the weight
of it] and He will sustain you; He will never allow
the [consistently] righteous to be moved (made to
slip, fall, or fail).

Psalm 55:22 AMP

NOVEMBER 1

You are the apple of God's eye and
He loves you more than you will
ever know. Believe it!

Keep me as the apple of the eye, hide me under the
shadow of thy wings,

Psalm 17:8 KJV

NOVEMBER 2

{
You are extremely valuable to God –
you are priceless!
}

Forasmuch as ye know that ye were not redeemed
with corruptible things, as silver and gold, from
your vain conversation received by tradition from
your fathers; But with the precious blood of Christ,
as of a lamb without blemish and without spot:

1 Peter 1:18 – 19 KJV

NOVEMBER 3

{
Choose to believe that God's grace
is enough to cover and sustain you.
His power is made perfect in
weakness.
}

For it is by grace you have been saved, through faith—and this is not from yourselves, it is the gift of God.

Ephesians 2:8 KJV

NOVEMBER 4

$$\left(\begin{array}{c}\text{Believe that God will never forsake}\\\text{you and He will meet the needs of}\\\text{your children.}\end{array}\right)$$

I have been young, and now am old; yet have I not seen the righteous forsaken, nor his seed begging bread.

Psalm 37:25 KJV

NOVEMBER 5

> This new day moves you one day
> closer to your breakthrough!

This is the day the LORD has made. We will rejoice
and be glad in it.

Psalm 118:24 NLT

NOVEMBER 6

You may not be able to see your way, but you can believe your way.

(For we walk by faith, not by sight:)

2 Corinthians 5:7 KJV

NOVEMBER 7

Now would be a good time to give God some praise for the things He has done in your life! Hallelujah!

The Lord lives! Praise be to my Rock! Exalted be my God, the Rock, my Savior!

2 Samuel 22:47 NIV

NOVEMBER 8

The way has already been made for you because your Father is the King. Embrace whose you are!

I will go before thee, and make the crooked places straight.

Isaiah 45:2 KJV

NOVEMBER 9

You are a child of the One True
Living God, which means you are
not defeated – victory belongs to
you!

But to all who believed him and accepted him, he
gave the right to become children of God.

John 1:12 NLT

NOVEMBER 10

> Whatever you do, do it all to the glory of God.

Whether therefore ye eat, or drink, or whatsoever ye do, do all to the glory of God.

1 Corinthians 10:31 KJV

[315]

NOVEMBER 11

God doesn't limit the number of
times you can come to Him to
obtain mercy, but you must come in
order to obtain it. Acknowledge
your need and ask Him for help.

For the Lord God is our sun and our shield. He
gives us grace and glory. The Lord will withhold
no good thing from those who do what is right.

Psalm 84:11 NLT

NOVEMBER 12

To "delight" means to experience great joy in God's presence. You will be delighted when you understand God's great love for you. Commit everything to the Lord, and believe that He can take care of you better than you can.

Delight thyself also in the LORD: and he shall give thee the desires of thine heart.

Psalm 37:4 KJV

NOVEMBER 13

Don't be afraid because the enemy is planning your demise – God is going to strategically use that same plan to elevate you.

They dig a deep pit to trap others, then fall into it themselves.

Psalm 7:15 NLT

NOVEMBER 14

{
God has a plan for your life!
Prosperity!
}

You can make many plans, but the Lord's purpose will prevail.

Proverbs 19:21 NLT

NOVEMBER 15

Do you need strength and peace today?

The LORD will give strength unto his people; the LORD will bless his people with peace.

Psalm 29:11 KJV

NOVEMBER 16

{ Jesus loves you sooo much that He
died for you! Jesus loves you! }

When we were utterly helpless, Christ came at just
the right time and died for us sinners.

Romans 5:6 NLT

NOVEMBER 17

$$\left\{ \begin{array}{c} \text{You were not born to be normal,} \\ \text{mediocre, or average; you were born} \\ \text{to be great!} \end{array} \right\}$$

Ye have not chosen me, but I have chosen you, and ordained you, that ye should go and bring forth fruit, and that your fruit should remain:

John 15:16a KJV

NOVEMBER 18

No one whose hope is in God will
ever be put to shame.

Yea, let none that wait on thee be ashamed: let them
be ashamed which transgress without cause.

Psalm 25:3 KJV

NOVEMBER 19

We are more than conquerors
through Him that loved us. Believe
and receive it!

Nay, in all these things we are more than
conquerors through him that loved us.

Romans 8:37 KJV

NOVEMBER 20

If God be for you, who can be against you? Not your enemies; not your haters; not your boss; not the doctor's report; not the mortgage company; and certainly not "the man"!

See, I have engraved you on the palms of my hands.

Isaiah 49:16 NIV

NOVEMBER 21

God's Spirit joins Himself to our spirits to declare we are God's children. Since we are His children, we will possess the blessings He keeps for His people, and we will also possess with Christ what God has kept for Him.

The Spirit itself beareth witness with our spirit, that we are the children of God: And if children, then heirs; heirs of God, and joint-heirs with Christ; if so be that we suffer with him, that we may be also glorified together.

Romans 8:16 – 17 KJV

NOVEMBER 22

God gives assurances of His strength, help, and victory over sin and death. Are you aware of the many ways God has helped you?

Fear thou not; for I am with thee: be not dismayed; for I am thy God: I will strengthen thee; yea, I will help thee; yea, I will uphold thee with the right hand of my righteousness.

Isaiah 41:10 KJV

NOVEMBER 23

Peace with God is possible only because Jesus paid the price for you through His death on the cross.

Therefore being justified by faith, we have peace with God through our Lord Jesus Christ:

Romans 5:1 KJV

NOVEMBER 24

$$\Big(\text{You are the righteousness of God.}$$
Not because you worked for it, but
you believe God and accepted His
gift of love.

But to him that worketh not, but believeth on him
that justifieth the ungodly, his faith is counted for
righteousness.

Romans 4:5 KJV

NOVEMBER 25

FAMILY REUNION:
Now is the time to let go of your
unforgiveness, bitterness, and
grudges. God wants to heal your
family! Do you want to hold on to
these things or do you want to hold
on to your love ones?

And he shall turn the heart of the fathers to the
children, and the heart of the children to their
fathers, lest I come and smite the earth with a curse.

Malachi 4:6 KJV

NOVEMBER 26

$\Big($ May you be made strong with all the
strength which comes from His
glorious power. $\Big)$

Be on your guard; stand firm in the faith; be
courageous; be strong.

1 Corinthians 16:13 NIV

NOVEMBER 27

THE LAST LAUGH:
You may be crying now because
they don't appreciate who you are or
because of your current situation,
but God is going to give you the last
laugh!

Blessed are ye that hunger now: for ye shall be filled. Blessed are ye that weep now: for ye shall laugh.

Luke 6:21 KJV

NOVEMBER 28

{
MY EYES DON'T CRY
NO MORE:
The nights of crying your eyes out
give way to days of laughter.
}

For his anger endureth but a moment; in his favour is life: weeping may endure for a night, but joy cometh in the morning.

Psalm 30:5 KJV

NOVEMBER 29

Your present troubles are small and
won't last very long.

For our light affliction, which is but for a moment,
worketh for us a far more exceeding and eternal
weight of glory;

2 Corinthians 4:17 KJV

[334]

NOVEMBER 30

Blessings and prosperity will be yours!

Blessed is every one that feareth the LORD; that walketh in his ways. For thou shalt eat the labour of thine hands: happy shalt thou be, and it shall be well with thee.

Psalm 128:1 – 2 KJV

DECEMBER 1

$$\left\{ \begin{array}{c} \text{Those who trust in the Lord are like} \\ \text{Mount Zion, which cannot be} \\ \text{shaken.} \end{array} \right\}$$

They that trust in the LORD shall be as mount Zion, which cannot be removed, but abideth for ever.

Psalm 125:1 KJV

[336]

DECEMBER 2

You may be lonely, but you are never alone. Jesus gave you the following promise:

I will not leave you comfortless: I will come to you.

John 14:18 KJV

DECEMBER 3

Sometimes, what looks like a
disappointment is simply God
getting us into a position to see His
greatness. Don't let
DISAPPOINTMENT distract you
from your APPOINTMENT with a
miracle!

For Sarah conceived, and bare Abraham a son in his
old age, at the set time of which God had spoken to
him.

Genesis 21:2 KJV

DECEMBER 4

RENEWED STRENGTH:
Are you tired? Tired of trying to
start a business, tired of dealing
with an illness, tired of raising a
difficult child, tired of being lonely
while waiting to meet the right
person...tired of waiting on the
promises of God?

But they that wait upon the LORD shall renew their
strength; they shall mount up with wings as eagles;
they shall run, and not be weary; and they shall
walk, and not faint.

Isaiah 40:31 KJV

DECEMBER 5

$$\Bigg\lbrace \text{Whenever you become tired, wait on the Lord and He will renew your strength.} \Bigg\rbrace$$

Blessed are all who wait for him!

Isaiah 30:18 NIV

DECEMBER 6

{
God is the source, and we are to be
the resource that He uses to bless
someone in need. Be a blessing!
}

Everything was created through him and for him.

Colossians 1:16 NLT

DECEMBER 7

{
For God so loved YOU that He gave
His only begotten Son.
}

For God so loved the world, that he gave his only
begotten Son, that whosoever believeth in him
should not perish, but have everlasting life.

John 3:16 KJV

DECEMBER 8

$$\left(\begin{array}{c} \text{What can God do for you? God is a} \\ \text{faithful God, and He always delivers} \\ \text{on time.} \end{array}\right)$$

He delivers your soul from death, your eyes from tears, and your feet from stumbling,

Psalm 116:8 NIV

DECEMBER 9

When the enemy comes in like a flood, let him know he can't win because the tomb is empty.

He is not here; he has risen, just as he said. Come and see the place where he lay.

Matthew 28:6 NIV

[344]

DECEMBER 10

{
Jesus got up – so why are you
looking down? Keep your head up,
the Lord will take care of your
situation!
}

But God raised him from the dead, freeing him
from the agony of death, because it was impossible
for death to keep its hold on him.

Acts 2:24 NIV

DECEMBER 11

When Jesus entered Jerusalem, the whole city was moved or "shaken." And when Jesus enters your life, there's a "shaking." He'll shake up everything in your life and remove those things that can be shaken, so that what cannot be shaken may remain.

And when he was come into Jerusalem, all the city was moved, saying, Who is this?

Matthew 21:10 KJV

[346]

DECEMBER 12

{
Jesus reigns. And as the Son, He
Shines! Allow the Son shine and
reign to change your life like never
before.
}

Therefore the Lord himself shall give you a sign;
Behold, a virgin shall conceive, and bear a son, and
shall call his name Immanuel.

Isaiah 7:14 KJV

DECEMBER 13

$$\left\{\begin{array}{c} \text{Do not despise small beginnings.} \\ \text{God does His best work through} \\ \text{small things!} \end{array}\right\}$$

For who hath despised the day of small things? for they shall rejoice, and shall see the plummet in the hand of Zerubbabel with those seven; they are the eyes of the LORD, which run to and fro through the whole earth.

Zechariah 4:10 KJV

DECEMBER 14

$$\left\{ \begin{array}{c} \text{When God closes a door, He raises} \\ \text{the roof. Take the limits off of God!} \end{array} \right\}$$

How often they rebelled against him in the wilderness and grieved him in the wasteland! Again and again they put God to the test; they vexed the Holy One of Israel. They did not remember his power— the day he redeemed them from the oppressor.

Psalm 78:40 – 42 NIV

DECEMBER 15

Wisdom will keep you safe from
those who will attempt to lure you
off the path that God has set for your
life.

Do not forsake wisdom, and she will protect you;
love her, and she will watch over you.

Proverbs 4:6 NIV

DECEMBER 16

Don't underestimate God if you want to receive the promise He has for your life.

For as the heavens are higher than the earth, so are my ways higher than your ways, and my thoughts than your thoughts.

Isaiah 55:9 KJV

DECEMBER 17

God expects us to love Him with all
our heart!

Jesus replied, "'You must love the Lord your God
with all your heart, all your soul, and all your mind.

Matthew 22:37 NLT

DECEMBER 18

Adversity strengthens your faith –
stick with the Lord through it all!

But by means of their suffering, he rescues those
who suffer. For he gets their attention through
adversity.

Job 36:15 NLT

DECEMBER 19

$$\left\{ \begin{array}{c} \text{If you need additional resources,} \\ \text{faith opens the door to new} \\ \text{resources. Believe God!} \end{array} \right\}$$

For God is the one who provides seed for the farmer and then bread to eat. In the same way, he will provide and increase your resources and then produce a great harvest of generosity in you.

2 Corinthians 9:10 NLT

DECEMBER 20

When you let go, God will take over.
Trust Him!

Those who trust in themselves are fools, but those who walk in wisdom are kept safe.

Proverbs 28:26 NIV

DECEMBER 21

How do you keep your head up
during difficult times? Look up to
the One who can change the times.
Have a blessed day!

I lift up my eyes to you, to you whose throne is in
heaven.

Psalm 123:1 NIV

DECEMBER 22

The tongue is a powerful weapon.
Let's be careful what we say –
someone's life may depend on it!

Death and life are in the power of the tongue.

Proverbs 18:21 KJV

DECEMBER 23

You no longer have to be bound.
Enjoy your freedom in Christ!

Now the Lord is the Spirit, and where the Spirit of
the Lord is, there is freedom.

2 Corinthians 3:17 NIV

DECEMBER 24

Under the Constitution we have life, liberty, and the pursuit of happiness. Under the Kingdom of God we have life more abundantly.

For the kingdom of God is not meat and drink; but righteousness, and peace, and joy in the Holy Ghost.

Romans 14:17 KJV

DECEMBER 25

> May the God of hope fill you with all joy and peace as you trust in Him, so that you may overflow with hope by the power of the Holy Spirit.

Now the God of hope fill you with all joy and peace in believing, that ye may abound in hope, through the power of the Holy Ghost.

Romans 15:13 NIV

DECEMBER 26

$$\left(\begin{array}{c} \text{You may not get what you wish for,} \\ \text{but you will get what you work for!} \\ \text{Be diligent!} \end{array}\right)$$

We want each of you to show this same diligence to the very end, so that what you hope for may be fully realized.

Hebrews 6:11 NIV

DECEMBER 27

Sometimes you need to change the way you talk to YOU about YOU. You are what you speak to yourself.

For as he thinketh in his heart, so is he.

Proverbs 23:7 KJV

DECEMBER 28

God is eternal, so He cannot speak a temporary word. Whatever He spoke over your life will surely come to pass!

Only I can tell you the future before it even happens. Everything I plan will come to pass.

Isaiah 46:10 NLT

DECEMBER 29

$$\Big\{ \text{The kind of faith you need today is:} \\ \text{"AT THY WORD"} \\ \text{faith.} \Big\}$$

The kind of faith you need today is:
"AT THY WORD"
faith.

And Simon answering said unto him, Master, we have toiled all the night, and have taken nothing: nevertheless at thy word I will let down the net.

Luke 5:5 KJV

DECEMBER 30

We've been defensive against the enemy for far too long. It's time to go on the offensive – it's time to take back EVERYTHING he stole.

And David enquired at the LORD, saying, Shall I pursue after this troop? shall I overtake them? And he answered him, Pursue: for thou shalt surely overtake them, and without fail recover all.

1 Samuel 30:8 NIV

DECEMBER 31

Your best days are yet to come!

Though thy beginning was small, yet thy latter end should greatly increase.

Job 8:7 KJV

Finally, my brethren, be strong in the Lord, and in the power of his might.

Ephesians 6:10 KJV

```
┌                              ┐
        DECLARE THIS:
  "I'm a work in progress. God is not
  through with me yet. God will finish
  what He started in my life!" Amen!

└                              ┘
```

Philippians 1:6 KJV

I am certain that God, who began the good work within you, will continue His work until it is finally finished on the day when Christ Jesus returns.

RANDOLPH E. DANIELS, SR.

In obedience to God, Pastor Daniels established *The Embassy of Grace* in 2011; in Orlando, Florida. This ministry was birthed out of a vision and a burden for individuals who are hurting, broken, wounded and uninspired, and are looking for help. While meeting the needs of the people, Pastor Daniels takes advantage of every opportunity to introduce them to the gospel of Jesus Christ, as well as help them establish or maintain a relationship built on faith, in Christ.

Daniels operates in the apostolic five-fold ministry, where he recognizes all gifts in the Body of Christ; men and women anointed as Apostles, Prophets, Evangelists, Pastors and Teachers.

He received his M.B.A. in International Business from Keller Graduate School of Management in 2011, and is seeking his Doctorate Degree in Theology. He lives in Orlando, Florida with his wife, Prophetess Daisy S. Daniels. They have three children: Ronald, DaiSha, and Randolph Jr.

TO CONTACT THE AUTHOR

Write: Randolph E. Daniels, Sr.
P.O. BOX 621433
Orlando, FL 32862
Telephone: (708) 704-6117
Email: theembassyofgrace@aol.com
Website:
www.thewritingonthewal.wix.com/daisysdaniels

THE WRITING ON THE WALL
PUBLISHING SERVICES

The Writing on the Wall Publishing Services is a Christian publishing house that is committed to excellence in Christian-theme publications.

The Writing on the Wall Publishing Services' goal is to equip you with the tools needed to successfully write, publish, and print your intellectual property, which will allow you to minister to the nations and advance the Kingdom of God. Our services include:

- MANUSCRIPT REVIEW
- MANUSCRIPT DEVELOPMENT / CONSULTING
- PAGE DESIGN AND LAYOUT
- COVER DESIGN
- ISBN NUMBER / BOOKLAND EAN BARCODE
- PRINTING
- COPYRIGHT

For more information, contact us:

Write: The Writing on the Wall Publishing Services
     P.O. BOX 621433
     Orlando, FL 32862 – 1433
Telephone: (708) 704-6117
Website: www.thewritingonthewal.wix.com/daisysdaniels
Email: thewritingonthewall@aol.com

[370]

www.ingramcontent.com/pod-product-compliance
Lightning Source LLC
Chambersburg PA
CBHW062358090426
42740CB00010B/1329